FIXING BRITAIN

This is one of the most remarkable people I have ever come across. His commitment, his dedication and his enthusiasm are quite extraordinary. He is a great British patriot.

Tony Blair, as Prime Minister
CBI Annual Dinner, May 2006

They broke the mould when he was made.

Sir John Sunderland,
Chairman Cadbury PLC, March, 2006

My friend Digby is a well-informed patriot who has 'been there and done it'. From early, cautionary tales about the impact that democratised markets in eastern Europe would have on the motor industry in his beloved West Midlands, to his warnings that India and China would 'have your lunch and your dinner', he is a trend spotter to keep Governments and commentators on their toes. This book is his catechism and his route map for taking the UK forward to where he believes it should be, and should never have slipped from.

Alastair Stewart OBE,
ITV News

FIXING BRITAIN

THE BUSINESS OF
RESHAPING OUR NATION

DIGBY JONES

WITH MICHAEL WILSON

A John Wiley and Sons, Ltd, Publication

ISBN 978-0-470-97763-7 (Hardback), ISBN 978-0-470-97924-2 (ebook)

ISBN 978-0-470-97925-9 (ebook), ISBN 978-1-119-97654-7 (ebook)

A catalogue record for this book is available from the British Library.

Set in 12pt Minion Pro by Sparks – www.sparkspublishing.com
Printed in Great Britain by TJ International Ltd, Padstow, Cornwall

To

Bernard Lowe, my primary school head teacher, who set me on my way.

John Webber, my headmaster at Bromsgrove, who fired my enthusiasm.

Jim Stephens, my tutor at University College, London, who developed my legal ability.

Gil Hayward, my Principal at Edge & Ellison, for answering all those questions and advising me along the way.

John Wardle, Senior Partner at Edge & Ellison when I joined in 1978 until 1990, for his inspiration and example.

Sir Clive Thompson, President of the CBI, 1999 and 2000, for giving me the break that changed my life.

My mother and father for all the love, encouragement and enthusiasm I could ever have wished for.

My wife, Pat. Simply my rock.

CONTENTS

CHAPTER 1

FIVE MINUTES TO MIDNIGHT – TIME FOR CHANGE

Consider, for a moment, a small country which ventured out from a place rather distant from the rest of the world but which proceeded to create the most powerful economic and military empire the world had ever seen.

It gave the world a common language, a common currency, the rule of law, the freedom of citizenship, tariff-free trade and peace. But after that amazing achievement, in the space of just three or four generations, it was all over.

I speak, of course, of Rome.

But Rome's majestic achievement declined and collapsed, alarmingly and quickly.

Rome didn't fall apart because the Huns came out of the Ardennes Forest or the Scots came over Hadrian's Wall. Rome fell apart in Rome. It became complacent, lazy, and indolent. Its citizens stopped caring for each other. It became a society for the selfish. Its people concentrated on their rights, not their responsibilities. As it unknowingly approached its own demise, it lacked leadership and blamed everyone but itself.

We all know that Rome wasn't built in a day but, relatively speaking, it fell apart in an afternoon.

I don't want that to happen to my country.

***

I have an essential creed for business's role in our society – my country.

I have always believed in socially inclusive wealth creation; skilling a dynamic and confident workforce and letting them enjoy the rewards of ability and sheer hard work, instead of allowing yet another generation to be consigned to valueless obscurity by a society and a system that simply doesn't care – or perhaps even worse, doesn't know what it's destroying.

Over the past decade or so, I've seen at first hand how political dogmatism, the making of policy in ignorance of real life, and an inability to harness the good of business can lead to the disintegration of a cohesive society. And I'm not sure now that 'society' – whatever that is – has the tools, the knowledge or the will to learn how to put itself back together.

We are the sixth biggest manufacturing country on earth. As you read this book, there's probably an Airbus flying from Santiago in Chile to Sao Paulo in Brazil, or from Chicago to San Francisco, or from Cape Town to Johannesburg. Approximately half of each of those planes is built in Britain. The wings are built in Broughton in North Wales. The undercarriages made in Gloucester. Many of the avionics are made by small businesses in the North and Midlands. Under the wings are the best engines you will find anywhere in the world, made by Rolls Royce in Derby. The Germans, the Spanish and the French all make a sizeable contribution but the bits that are important, the bits that get it up there, keep it up there and bring it safely down again, are all made in the UK.

Our country has declined to a such a state that is in serious need of fixing, but we do have the framework on which to base our fightback.

The most productive car plant in the whole of Europe, the second most productive in the world, is Nissan's plant in Sunderland. Where is the only other place in Europe where Toyota is building its hybrid car? Burnaston in Derbyshire. Not France nor Germany – but in Britain. The UK is home to some 70% of the Formula One motor racing teams, the second most watched sport on earth. They are not here for the fun of it but for the high-class engineering skills they find in Britain – even Michael Schumacher's Mercedes is built in Northampton!

We are a globally preferred place for food manufacture and export. The second biggest pharmaceutical company in the world, GlaxoSmithKline is based in West London.

Our creative industries generate thousands of millions of pounds in web design, textile design, books, film, art, theatre, architecture, advertising, consultant engineering. A British consulting engineer delivered the Birds Nest stadium at the 2008 Beijing Olympics, and the Watercube, where all those swimming records were broken. A British architect designed the spectacular suspension bridge across the Tarn River Gorge in France.

Of the top ten universities in the world, four are English – Cambridge, Oxford, University College and Imperial College, London. If you look at the top one hundred universities in the world, the only country with more than us is America. Our higher education system is first class – a status achieved almost in spite of, rather than because of, ourselves.

We don't celebrate what we're good at. We merely look inward and criticise all the time. We have ceased to believe that we do all this. The tragedy is that we have ceased to believe in ourselves.

> **We don't celebrate what we're good at. We merely look inward and criticise all the time.**

Here, business gets on the agenda merely through gloom or facile entertainment. Fifty redundancies at a manufacturer makes the headlines, not the fact that Jaguar has had one of its most successful quarters. At the height of the recession it was so difficult, almost impossible, to get the nation's own broadcaster, the BBC, to cover the many good news business stories. The self-belief of the nation was debilitated again and again by the accurate but unbalanced constant drip, drip of bad news. Indeed, many small businesses told me that their only two good weeks in 2008 were those when Obama's election and swine flu took the recession off the top slot on the *Ten O'Clock News*.

And business gets a hostile handling from the TV entertainment media. In *Coronation Street*, *EastEnders* and even *The Archers*, when a crook surfaces in a soap storyline, yes, he's a businessman. In another TV show, Alan Sugar gets out of his Rolls Royce and tells some unfortunates that 'You're fired'. Which business in modern Britain is run like that? How simplistic and how damaging that is to society's expectations and understanding of essential wealth creation.

But despite all our success, this nation is at a crossroads. We've come out of a severe recession and with good, firm economic management we will survive it, but the real poverty is one of expectation. The real depression in this country is not economic, it is the decline in talent, sadly something over which the last government presided. The real worry is that the damage to social cohesion, the destruction of the glue of our society, is permanent.

We need some plain thinking, plain talking and action.

Government intrusion has complicated running a business, teaching a class, employing more people, taking a risk and simply doing a job. Incompetence in government delivery has left us all poorer. And there's been a poverty of straightforward and honest planning for the good of UK PLC. It has been easier for government to fashion its own layers of bureaucracy, to intervene and appear to be doing something than to take the more difficult route to plain, simple and effective solutions. Much of this is because few of our politicians have had any experience of real life, or a real job.

But I believe we can fix this country – economically, yes – but, far more importantly, make it a greater place for families who are trying to bring up their children into society, helping them get good jobs, and lead fulfilling lives, and in so doing, help our country achieve twenty-first century success.

At the root of it all is the desperate state of our education system. Tony Blair promised 'Education, education, education'. We got a scholastic generation who are not equipped for the world of work. Employers complain that, even after A level studies, many school leavers have basic problems with literacy and numeracy and seem to think that the world owes them a living.

Employers also complain that there are growing questions about the whole system, as exams get easier. More students are getting higher grades. The education bosses are saying, correctly in part, that this shows how much better education is. The first users of the educated product, the first employers of these students, disagree. They see an increase over time of academic grades much more quickly than any real increase in academic standards.

This 'grade inflation' is having a miraculous effect but it merely, as does all inflation, devalues capital. In this case, the capital of education. For example, at the current rate of academic 'improvement', in nine years' time no one sitting an A-level will fail the exam – and over those nine years, a third of those sitting them will get A grades. This is not an education system for the fifth largest economy in the world. The brightest aren't being stretched, and others are appearing to be better prepared than they really are.

Our basic education system is flawed, not only in its inability to teach literacy and numeracy, but to send students into employment with a realistic measure of their competence. If that doesn't change then UK PLC will be bypassed by the many other nations which are hungrier and better equipped to teach their young people about the real world.

***

So, what kind of a country do we live in? Our main 'community' – if you take that to mean an area within which people are connected – is the social media. By July 2010, Facebook had notched up 25 million members in the UK, meaning that just over one in two citizens was a part of the site. It connects over 500 million people worldwide. It's therefore not unreasonable to take Facebook as representing a coalition of opinion, if its members decide on a common issue. Which many of them did in 2010; thousands posted sympathetic messages to offer support to the memory of the wife-beating, murdering thug Raoul Moat.

Why would those people sympathise with a monster like that?

Maybe, if you look beyond Moat's wickedness and the 'sympathy' expressed online, you find a rather bleak territory. Moat's rampage was, thankfully, an exceptional act, but he clearly touched a deep nerve in those thousands who posted their support. If you are white, male and possibly unemployed, but you're healthy, you're able-bodied and you're living in a rather challenged environment, possibly where you don't hear the English language spoken in the street very often, you may well feel that the political class has completely and absolutely ignored you. And you may also feel that no one out there is shouting for you, which is why extreme political parties like the BNP have such purchase. All they have to do to get a foothold is to prey on that insecurity and anger which our broken society and system have caused.

No doubt some of Moat's support also came from an inbred hatred of the police, who seem powerless to stop crime, and are also, no matter how unfairly, simply seen as the enemy.

That dislocation and lack of direction, anger and perhaps despair is not helped by the country's benefit culture. There have been some great social advances over the past sixty years – the NHS is the obvious one, the welfare benefit system helps many people who are disabled and out of work, as does the National Minimum Wage, and Health and Safety legislation for those in work.

But the effect of state protection and intervention has been to encourage a 'gimme' society, in which people can simply say, 'I have no responsibilities but I do have rights. So I don't need to worry

The effect of state protection and intervention has been to encourage a 'gimme' society, in which people can simply say, 'I have no responsibilities but I do have rights.'

about anything, "they" will provide'. And when the tap is turned off, that's when the trouble starts.

There was a mantra amongst many so-called New Labour ministers of 'there, there, here's some money'. I've lost count of the number of times I have heard politicians say that of course they don't agree with state handouts; but the flow of benefits has continued for years with little oversight and no real strategy as to its long-term purpose. Of course, if you constantly give people money – and let's not forget that this is essentially other people's hard-earned cash – you run the very real risk of nurturing a sense of entitlement that removes any incentive for people to take responsibility socially or to start earning for themselves.

Frequently I see local authorities try to work out ways of getting people out of broken, welfare-bound housing estates, where practically no one works. But then you hear teenage girls saying, 'I want to get pregnant because if I do, I'll get a council house'. And even in the world of work, employers face resistance from employees who fear being promoted because a pay rise means a loss of state benefit.

These things should not be acceptable in the fifth largest economy on earth, as we face the huge, competitive challenge of globalisation.

To modify the old cliché somewhat – if you give people fish every day, you'll be giving them fish every day for the rest of their lives. However, if you buy them a fishing boat, teach them to fish and take them to the fishing grounds, you won't have to buy them fish ever again.

But, over the past couple of decades the country has, through a political quest for popularity and misguided theory, created a benefit culture which feeds on itself, stifles any aspirations of work or development of self-worth and which will take a generation to reverse, such is its systemic inertia.

***

And if work is, rather unsurprisingly, a sustainable route out of poverty and benefit, why is that thinking also not applied to those on the lowest rung – the prison population?

There are 60 million people in this country and we have a prison population of 85,000. We have the worst reoffending rate in the whole of Europe. Among the younger prisoners, 95% will reoffend and go back inside – in Denmark the figure is 45%, in the Netherlands it is 55% and, even in the US, it's 'only' about 36% according to the European Society of Criminology. The cost of the crime, the cost to the judicial system and the cost of their imprisonment is, on average, a quarter of a million pounds every time. To me that seems a staggering burden to the taxpayer.

Multiply that by 85,000 and it quickly becomes apparent why it is in society's interests to find ways to ensure that each and every £250,000 isn't just a sunk cost. What's more, it's paramount that that prisoner does not reoffend and in turn invoice the taxpayer for £500,000 and rising.

Never mind the pointless recidivism. We, as a society, actually pay prisoners to do menial tasks that require no skill and have little value. It is right and proper that we pay prisoners wages, but their 'work' is not usually of the value-added kind. So we end up paying prisoners more money for worthless tasks than if they had elected to learn to read, write and count and operate a computer – which is, of course, the only way they're ever going to get a job when they get out of prison.

It is an indictment of the real poverty in twenty-first century Britain that just 0.14% of the population can cost the country billions of pounds – and also such distress and insecurity. It goes to show just how much social cohesion has fallen apart.

***

At the same time, we have schools which are delivering young people who are unfit for the world of work after 11 years of full-time, free, compulsory education. How many young people in other parts of the world would love to have that privilege? The statistics are simply dreadful.

I first came across them in 2000. I had been at the CBI for only a couple of months and I was to give a speech on the importance of training and education. I read an influential report by Sir Claus Moser on Britain's fitness for purpose in the twenty-first century. This is what I saw:

> *Some seven million adults in England – one in five adults – if given the alphabetical index to the* Yellow Pages, *cannot locate the page reference for plumbers. That is an example of functional illiteracy. It means that one in five adults has less literacy than is expected of an 11-year-old child. These figures – based on official surveys – are inevitably estimates, and may be a little on the high side: but the order of magnitude is certainly right.*

> *The situation for numeracy is both worse and more confusing because the tests are weaker and the evidence is controversial. Estimates of the percentage of adults having some numeracy problems range from 30% to 50%.*

After simple disbelief, my next thought was, 'And we want to take on China and India, do we? Don't make me laugh.' And then the anger set in at this staggering statistic about my country, which has not left me to this day.

Since this report was published we've had the even more depressing evidence that half the children who take their GCSEs do not get grade C or above in English or Maths – which means

People who aren't skilled are those who are ill-equipped to deal with the effects of globalisation, and are left behind in the shift to a value-added, innovative economy. that after 11 years of free, full-time education, from a government which promised teaching as a high priority – these sixteen-year-olds are not fit for working in a global competitive economy outside the playground.

And only last August figures were published that 20% of 11-year-olds remain functionally illiterate and innumerate. In late 2010 the government reiterated that this disgraceful figure is not improving. So the scandal continues. 'Education, education, education', Mr Blair? I think not!

The consequences of this are obvious and inevitable. People who aren't skilled are those who are ill-equipped to deal with the effects of globalisation, and are left behind in the shift to a value-added, innovative economy. Their only future is to lose self-respect and self-esteem and, soon enough, the man selling the white powder at the end of the street appears to have the answer. Then the mugging and theft to pay for that begins, with appalling consequences for all of us.

When these people have children of their own, often as teenagers themselves, there are no books in the home. Why have books at home if no one reads? So, with no learning and no desire for improvement, this underclass develops on its own, and that spirals into this overdependency on the welfare state.

This lack of education, this failed system of learning, is of such enormous and shocking proportions that it's an obscenity, a blight on our nation.

Just as the latest scholastic generation was beginning its time at school, in 1997, the new Prime Minister Tony Blair was promising education, education, education.

Yet what we got at the end of it was ignorance, failure and unemployability.

***

What a wasted opportunity! Tony Blair and Gordon Brown came into power taking over from a stale, tired, ideologically corrupt administration. Even some Tories said to me that they thought they would do well, and there was a reservoir of goodwill in the country even from those who didn't vote for them. But, frankly, they wasted so much.

I'm moved to a wry smile when I remember the 'memoir fest' of the summer of 2010, from Campbell, Mandelson and then Blair.

If only they'd spent a lot more of the energy, the emotionally draining time, the effort, the hours that they'd spent on fighting each other, on fixing the country instead, then we wouldn't be in half the mess we are in now.

Whatever you think of her, Margaret Thatcher set about changing the face of UK PLC – and she did just that. As a young lawyer in Birmingham in the 1980s I saw the improvement in efficiency and productivity in the West Midlands. The change was painful, certainly, but it forged companies who were fit to compete with the growing industrial strength of Asia.

But, much more than that, Thatcher saw how important inward investment was for manufacturing. Whilst, for example, our national car industry was busy committing suicide with appalling labour relations, poor management, low productivity and an awful mass-market range of cars, Japan was taking a lead, searching for new production opportunities. Britain offered inward investment when others were running scared of commercial immigration. Japanese car manufacturers were able to make the most of the new-found labour market flexibility in this country and, thankfully, the legacy exists to this day.

Nissan UK now has its most productive car plant in the whole of the world. Toyota is currently building its most important car at Burnaston. Honda has injected new life into the old railway town of Swindon. Business was Margaret Thatcher's constituency. She faced up to it, she challenged it, she reformed it – forever.

So when Labour came to power in 1997, I assumed that they would sort out their own constituency, the public sector – which even then was clearly out of control. And for five years it all went so well. Granting independence to the Bank of England; tight control of the public finances. 'Prudence' at every turn. 'A Labour government … a *Labour* government … (to borrow from Neil Kinnock), cutting capital gains tax to 10%. Middle England was getting what it voted for.

But I should have known better. In the 2002 Budget Gordon Brown announced the 1% National Insurance rise which took everyone, including us at the CBI, by complete surprise. I told him that night that he was putting more money into the Health Service and the other public sectors without asking them to reform. Brown's response to me was that they would reform, because they were being given the money!

I couldn't help but wonder that night just how those particular turkeys would be voting for Christmas. Tony Blair claimed that he wore 'the scars on my back' from trying to get these people to reform, but I still doubt the evidence of that. One of the reasons we have this bloated, inefficient, unproductive public sector is precisely due to a lack of reform and the sad consequence is our ballooning budget deficit which has nearly bankrupted us as a nation. The bankers, but certainly not all of them, made a disgraceful contribution to the meltdown, but no one should say that the public sector cuts are because of bankers'

> **One of the reasons we have this bloated, inefficient, unproductive public sector, is precisely due to a lack of reform and the sad consequence is our ballooning budget deficit which has nearly bankrupted us as a nation.**

errors of judgement and profligacy. As a nation we were paying for services in ways we could not afford from 2002 to 2009 and we borrowed to do it, because we couldn't afford it out of the money we as a country had earned. That had little to do with the banking crisis.

I despair when I learn that, as taxpayers, we employ a Bus Lane Infringement Adjudicator in Birmingham and a Street Naming Executive in Scotland, and when the number of administrators in the Health Service has gone up by a factor of eight in the last ten years, when in the same time, the number of nurses has only doubled.

I went to a hospital a few years ago, when I was at the CBI, and they praised the value of their cancer scanner, whose use naturally had a long waiting list. But the waiting list was long, not just because of the demand, but because manning hours and procedures meant that it didn't operate as efficiently as it could have done.

'This is a disgrace' I said. 'I will lobby hard to get this changed.' But one of the executives of the hospital said, 'No, don't do that, because we are fixing it next week. We've got more money from the government so we're going to halve the waiting list in a week … we're going to buy another machine!'.

The result? Public evidence of 'investment in the NHS'.

The headline that following week would have been, 'Extra Spending Halved the Waiting List'. Factually accurate, yes. Utterly and absolutely a waste of taxpayers money, certainly.

That's the crux of proper reform. Make more of the current assets and get the people, with fewer of them in the back office, to work more efficiently, not necessarily harder.

If someone had turned round and said 'I'm not buying another machine for that hospital but I'm going to make the existing machine work all day, seven days a week', then the next headlines would have screamed, 'Leave my NHS alone', or 'Sweat shop NHS'. But that would have been the answer and only a Blair government could have done that. More disappointingly, if Brown had put his clearly talented, supreme effort into it, it would have happened.

That is the huge frustration and today our nation is paying a price for it.

***

When I was leaving the CBI, I was asked what I thought was Blair's greatest achievement. I said it was Northern Ireland. I reckoned that he had picked up Major's legacy there, really made some difficult decisions and stuck at it – and as he once observed, if he could get a young Belfast kid through to adulthood without violence, we all stood a chance.

He pulled that off. How interesting it is that now the police refer to the occasional bad behaviour during the Orange Day parades as 'recreational rioting'.

Another, and most unexpected, of Blair's achievements was personal to me. He made me a supporter of fox-hunting! As a product of the urban West Midlands, instinctively I would have been against it, and I'd never think about picking up a gun, to shoot and kill a living creature for enjoyment.

But then, when I saw more parliamentary time spent on the issue of fox-hunting than on going to war in Iraq I realised this was not an issue but a symptom of a left wing struggle, which became very nasty. And when the Act banning it was passed I heard some politician being interviewed, who actually said, 'This is the last act of the Class War'.

I hoped that the listeners would realise that this had nothing to do with the fox at all, and everything to do with a political dogma. This disregard for the important and distinct community in rural Britain, showed that the government knew little and cared even less. Labour are essentially an urban party. Blair turned me from a fox-hunting anti, or probably agnostic, to a pro, and revealed a total disregard for democratic freedoms and the government's duty to govern for everyone and not just an urban politically and class motivated clique.

Fundamental to a democracy is the fact that the role of majority government is to hold the ring for a minority as long as that minority is not hurting other people. Majorities can look after themselves. The fox-hunting community was a minority which was a very important part of rural life. It created jobs and it brought in money – but more importantly it was about social cohesion, it was about the glue that kept a community together. And, at a stroke, from its urban bias, Labour destroyed it.

Fundamental to a democracy is the fact that the role of majority government is to hold the ring for a minority as long as that minority is not hurting other people.

I remember the famous verse which says:

> *In Germany they came first for the Communists, and I didn't speak up because I wasn't a Communist. Then they came for the Jews, and I didn't speak up because I wasn't a Jew. Then they came for the trade unionists, and I didn't speak up because I wasn't a trade unionist. Then they came for the Catholics, and I didn't speak up because I was a Protestant. Then they came for me, and by that time no one was left to speak up.'*

– Pastor Martin Niemöller, 1945

Not for a minute can anyone make a comparison with our open, democratic government (of whatever party) but it's the sentiment that strikes me as poignant. The atmosphere at the time felt as if a majority had turned against a minority in support of the politically expedient and I worried where that might stop. I felt let down. The nation deserved better. Was this the thin end of the wedge of state control becoming over-powerful and damagingly too intrusive in local communities?

None of it should have surprised me since I've seen politicians at first hand with no experience whatsoever of real life, passing laws and developing policy that they think is relevant. When I was a minister, I'd have advisers and they'd be 25 years old. Highly intelligent, they worked hard, but they'd never done anything with their lives, never been a teacher, never worked in a hospital, never worked in business, never accepted the responsibility of employing people and had never taken a risk. They were marking time until a parliamentary seat became free in whichever party they supported, where they hoped there was a big majority. Then the plan was to get adopted and get elected as an MP. Becoming whip-fodder, keeping their noses clean, the prize would be to become a minister – and shizzam! – they'd have power. But they'd never done *anything*. Governing the country with no experience of life at all!

***

I was particularly staggered by the attitude of one parliamentarian.

I had entered the House of Lords in 2007 and I learnt very quickly what a privilege it is to listen to some of the best minds in Britain and take part in shaping the country's laws. People who have done something with their lives, who are experts in their field. They don't override the Commons because there's no democratic connection in the Lords, but rather they inform the debate, revise or amend the legislation which governs us all. The nation gets a more independent and objective review of law-making and it's free!

The man who gave me the strongest affirmation of the House of Lords, though, was John Prescott. The arch Old Labourite, who'd been given the post of Deputy Prime Minister to Blair as a Machiavellian sop to the side of the Labour Party that hated modernism, spent a lot of his time lampooning the Lords.

After a governmental career of achieving little other than keeping Labour's left wing in line with Blair's 'third way', this class warrior caved in at the smell of ermine; 'Two Jags' Prezzer became Baron Prescott of Kingston upon Hull, with a seat on the red leather benches of the House of Lords. That was bad enough, but after his first exposure to the Lords' arena, he actually praised the Lords by stating he had sat in there for the first time and heard a world-renowned expert talking about a piece of pending legislation. I actually heard him say it was so informative and so good.

How can a Deputy Prime Minister, after thirteen years in power, have been so ignorant of the workings of the Upper House? Had he been blinded by tribalism and party dogma?

***

That's all fairly political, but here's the practical side of the sort of political ignorance which can ruin our country. For some time, I have proudly been an advisor to the very successful engineering company, JCB, a world-class brand. In the depths of the recession, this proud British company approached the department of the Business Minister, Peter Mandelson, asking for some short-term government support to keep their skilled workforce together. It's what a number of European countries do, including the Dutch, the French, the Belgians – the Germans even have a name for it, *kurzarbeit*, which means a short-term working scheme. It's finite and does not last as long as a downturn. The idea is that the skilled workers are kept on, but they only work for two or three days a week.

JCB proposed that, with the employees already agreeing to short-time working with one day a week unpaid, they would pay their skilled employees for two days a week, and that the government would pay another two days in which JCB would train the workers on other skills. The premise of their idea was to keep a reservoir of talent available *in situ* to take advantage of the inevitable upturn in the economy.

Mandelson turned them down, so JCB laid them off. Some of them became binmen in Derby. Now, there's nothing wrong with being a binman in Derby on a pension that the country can't afford. But now, with a modest upturn, JCB is entitled to ask where the skilled welders are that they need.

The worst thing is that if you are in a very safe job in a local authority, why are you going to resign and go back to an organisation where there is no guaranteed continuity of employment in a downturn? Every time there is a downturn you get laid off. And so next time there is a boom, JCB, like any other manufacturer in Britain, has a choice – they can make their diggers where there is a pool of skilled labour in India, or Brazil, or Shanghai … or Germany. What a loss that would be to our country.

***

When I declare that I am proud of my – our – country and I describe the heroes of mine that have formed a great nation, it is not a fashionable thing to say. If I were to start talking about this in a school today, too many teachers and administrators would accuse me of jingoism and demand that we should be apologetic about our past. I find that very difficult to understand.

We gave the world a common language, and an understanding of democracy, fair play and the importance of the rule of law. Of course we did some dreadful things, but we gave the world a common language, and an understanding of democracy, fair play and the importance of the rule of law, where everyone is equal before it. We made commerce a reality, and encouraged aspiration and self-esteem.

But I worry about how history is taught in school, if it's taught at all. No pupil should leave school until they've been round the Houses of Parliament and understand its relevance to him or her. I enjoy showing people around Westminster – and I'm often surprised at the ignorance of some people who should know better.

As I show them around and ask them 'who was the great commoner who, in amongst these kings and queens, lay in state in Westminster Hall?' they invariably say it was Lady Di. It was of course Sir Winston Churchill. More alarmingly, some people don't really know who he was. Now that is a disgrace! We cannot build a better future unless the next generation understands where we come from and how we got here.

I wonder as well if they'd know much about my other heroes, who provide huge insights into all the problems we face in life and the skills we need.

Nelson, for example. He trained his gunnery captains to a level of brilliance, of course, but he also delegated the detail of battle to the commanders of his ships. So they were confident in his delegation and trained to be nimble in their tactics. That was key to the battle, since the British captains were so different from the inflexible and authoritarian chains of command in the enemy, the French and Spanish fleets. His captains were effectively entrepreneurs working, under management they respected, towards a common objective and a well-communicated battle plan of strategic and tactical brilliance which they understood completely.

Using his highly skilled gun crews and confident chains of command he put in hand his winning and original battle plan at Trafalgar. Instead of having his ships go alongside the enemy and pound each other to pieces – the traditional way of naval engagement – he came bow-first straight into them. Innovatively, his ships had to endure unanswerable fire for a couple of hours to earn the opportunity to fire on undefended targets as they sailed through the enemy's lines. That was utterly different, courageous and crucial. He had prepared meticulously, he had trained his people, he had delegated authority, he had communicated effectively. He delivered. Lessons to be taken from our 'politically incorrect' history to be applied to so many walks of life.

Another British hero of mine is John Churchill, the First Duke of Marlborough. From humble beginnings he became a canny statesman and great military leader. The complexity of his political dealings makes Peter Mandelson look like an amateur. In 1704, through a combination of diplomacy and military tactical deception he marshalled the forces of the Grand Alliance and marched them halfway across Europe, down to Munich. There, at a place called Blindheim (Blenheim), in one afternoon, he destroyed the most powerful army in Europe, that of Louis XIV of France. In recognition of Churchill's achievements, Queen Anne gave him the Park of Woodstock in Oxfordshire. Here he built a house that has become seared into the national consciousness – Blenheim Palace.

Then, there's Winston Churchill himself. The greatest of inspirational figures, who held the nation together in its darkest moments. But how many times in the previous forty years did that man have to believe in himself, when everybody – *everybody* – doubted him?

In 1940 he had one single but nearly overwhelming task – to get our country to believe, to believe in itself, to believe the impossible was possible, to live 'we will never surrender' in all they spoke and did.

We are, of course, nationally short of figures like these. They come along at best once in a generation. But I think we can call on one common quality that could help our country out of its mess. We are natural traders, always have been. Islanders but with strong historical links to every part of the world. We instinctively understand how business works and should apply these instincts and principles to rectify what's gone wrong in Britain.

∗∗∗

I was born into business. Mum and dad owned a shop. When I was about seven or eight, I'd help behind the counter if one of them or my elder sister Cherryl had to pop off upstairs. When the deliveries came, I'd help unload them into the storeroom at the back. It was a very good introduction to the most basic type of business: retailing … and making a profit.

One day I was helping to serve and a customer came in for potatoes. They were a shilling a pound. As I bagged and then weighed them, they came in at just under a pound, so I put in an extra small potato which took the whole lot to just over a pound, but of course I only charged the woman the shilling. When she'd gone, dad said: 'You've just given my profit away'. I didn't understand, so he sat me down and explained the obvious. I'd given away his margin. Little did I know I had just learnt a fundamental lesson of retailing, of business.

My mum and dad would also tell me which items sold quickly and which would take their time to put cash back in the till – this was of course was my first introduction to cash flow.

On a Sunday afternoon, dad would show all the money he'd have to pay out and on the other side all the money he'd collected in. A very personal way to begin the practical side of the bookkeeping that I would later learn in detail.

My experience in the shop also taught me a difficult but highly valuable skill. How to deal with customers. Now millions of businesses, in shops or online, from banking to selling fashion, have to learn how to be 'customer facing'. But this was front line, relentless personal stuff. We were not a mighty supermarket.

As a corner shop we went beyond the old cliché about the 'customer is always right'. We understood our wider role in the community. The customer used us as a work whinge, marriage guidance counsellor, news service, football club confessional and local priest substitute – then they'd remember that they'd come in for five Woodbine cigarettes. We listened, we learned and of course we sold. 'Oh you'd better give me a box of those chocolates. I'll take it back to the wife', or 'oh I don't think we've got enough butter at home, bring me another pack'.

So, my understanding of the workings of business began on a very small scale and is infused in my blood – and I've never forgotten how important that was. A few decades on, when I became Director-General of the CBI, I was the first person they'd ever had in that role who'd actually been in a small business. They'd had some highly intelligent and incredibly clever people, but so many of them had never actually worked in the guts of a small business.

I also grew up next to a totem of local employment and wealth creation and realised how important local businesses are to the whole life of the community.

Most of the people who came into mum and dad's shop worked at the local Longbridge car factory – 'the Austin' as we all called it. It was a spanner's throw away and I began to understand the real dependence that a community has on the central genera-tor of employment. With us it was where they made Minis or Austin A40s – in South Yorkshire it would be the coal field, in Newcastle it would be the shipyard, in South Wales it would be the steelworks, in Manchester it would be the textile mill. Those different industries provided a similar central core to the com-munity and of course they've all gone, for many reasons – some good, some bad.

Replacing those totems, reinvigorating those communities – therein lies the challenge. The task is not to bemoan their pass-ing in a cry for yesterday, but to recognise the effects of their loss and deal with the fallout – both social and economic.

I have seen the breadth and the depth of Britain's working and non-working society. Whilst I was at the CBI and as Trade Min-ister I travelled to 70 countries. I have also seen how the rest of the world does it better. How hungry our overseas competition is, and how hard it's going to be for Britain to step up to the plate and deliver. Above all, after all those years, I am convinced of one thing – the power of business to make a difference. In fact to make *the* difference, to make a change for good – which could eventually prevent our country falling apart.

My days at the CBI gave me some clues on how business can – must – become a crucial part of our country's recovery and survival. For, as we stand today, the future is going to be very cold for Great Britain.

CHAPTER 2
THE VOICE OF BUSINESS

The Confederation of British Industry was founded in 1965 to lobby government on behalf of business. It was an amalgamation of the Federation of British Industries (FBI), the British Employers' Confederation (BEC) and the National Association of British Manufacturers. It created a national representative body of employers in the same way that the Trades Union Congress stood for the nation's unions, incorporating manufacturing, transport, construction and the then nationalised industries. The name sounds rather quaint today, with its evocation of portly businessmen from sooty metal-bashing industries, but its membership includes the UK's biggest companies from all sectors and from all over the world and it has a high profile unpaid chairman (or President) as well as the full-time CEO, or Director-General, to give it clout in the highest reaches of public decision making.

It operates regional offices around the UK with its headquarters in London. It is The Voice of Business from the small, owner-managed operation to the biggest multinational.

Our country depends upon the success of all of them. They are the crucial asset of Britain's balance sheet. They are our country's livelihood.

When you make money in a business, you can reward the shareholders with dividends, who pay tax on them, you can keep the cash in the business as retained profit and pay tax on it, or you can employ people and they pay tax on it. And that tax, in part, goes to pay the wages of all the public servants, the nurses, the teachers, the soldiers, the prison officers and the police. They of course pay tax on their incomes, but if there were no businesses in Britain there would be no tax. If it wasn't for the wealth created by UK PLC – large and small business alike – then there would be nothing to spend on schools and hospitals, on police officers, on soldiers, on nurses and on teachers. Only business generates taxation.

Because of that wealth creation, business is at the centre of Britain, more so than any other section of society.

And I have never thought that our society, and its opinion makers, from journalists to politicians, from environmentalists to trade unionists, get that fact and, if they do, they have a funny way of showing it!

So it has always struck me that, since wealth creation is so supremely important to our country, the CBI should shout that very loudly and at every opportunity.

'If the CBI didn't exist, someone would invent it', said a CBI member at my first President's Committee meeting. The nation needed a counterbalance to the overwhelming might of the trades unions who effectively ran Britain in the sixties and seventies. One of my formative moments was in 1976, hearing the democratically elected Chancellor of the Exchequer, Denis Healey, tell his electorate that if a gang of unelected, opaquely governed and unaccountable trades union officials would agree to wage demands of no more than 3%, he would reduce income tax by £1 billion a year. To me, as a law student at University College, London, it seemed as if the governance and fiscal running of the country was being

If it wasn't for the wealth created by UK PLC – large and small business alike – then there would be nothing to spend on schools and hospitals, on police officers, on soldiers, on nurses and on teachers. Only business generates taxation.

delegated to a vested interest that the country had never elected. As it happened the unions got their way and Healey agreed to a 4.5% wage claim. Not long after, the Chancellor had to go cap in hand to the IMF to bail our country out.

***

But all that was very far from my mind on a wet summer's evening in 1999 as I ran through the Botanical Gardens in Birmingham. I was late and on my way to an event that I knew was going to be my big night. But it was about to be the beginning of something bigger than I ever imagined.

I was Regional Chairman of the CBI, and on that June night, I was rushing to the annual summer banquet, for the West Midlands CBI.

I was to host the event and, coming up from London, were Sir Clive Thompson, the President of the CBI, and also a considerable businessman in his own right as Chief Executive of Rentokil PLC, and Baroness Jay, Margaret Jay, the Leader of the House of Lords.

It was the biggest public event in my career so far. In the eighties and nineties I was a corporate lawyer in the West Midlands, looking after a number of high profile businesses, at a time when the industries in the area were undergoing huge change as the pace of technological advance and international competitiveness either swept them along or caught them out. It was a very challenging stage of Britain's economic cycle; joining the CBI gave my firm, Edge & Ellison, a unique entrée into regional and national business policy, helping in advising our clients. I became the main liaison between my firm and the CBI, and in due course became more involved with the organisation. A few years later, I moved to a much larger firm, KPMG, as Vice-Chairman of Corporate Finance. It was around then that I was appointed, for two years, as unpaid non-executive Regional Chairman of the CBI in the West Midlands.

So, on that wet June night in 1999, in the Botanical Gardens, (where my wife Pat and I had held our wedding reception nine years before), a slightly damp Regional Chairman of the CBI, West Midlands, collected his thoughts.

There were going to be three speeches; mine, Sir Clive Thompson's and Baroness Jay's. As the host, mine was supposed to be something of a thank you to everyone for coming and then an introduction of the guests.

But then I thought, when am I ever again going to have a Cabinet minister and the President of the CBI as a captive audience?

So I stood up, and spoke to the room of 250 businessmen and women from the West Midlands about my vision. It came

And if business means anything as a force for good in this country, it is to reach out, down, round and under those who can't. straight from the heart, my vision for social inclusion and wealth creation, working together to make a difference to our society.

After appealing to the government to set business free, encourage us to create wealth and compete, to generate taxation and jobs, my final words were 'if you've really succeeded in business and you've made yourself a few bob, there's a nice car on the drive, your kids are in a good school, a nice holiday is coming up, but you've got razor wire on your boundary fences, your kids get mugged on their way home from school, and you get burgled on Friday night because we've forgotten to take the whole of society with us, what is the point? And if business means anything as a force for good in this country, it is to reach out, down, round and under those who can't. For those who won't – I'd stick an Exocet up their chuff personally – but for those who can't, we should be there for them. To be a force for good and to take them with us, to maximise their potential and help them achieve for themselves and for the country. Thank you for coming.' I sat down, to a big round of applause.

I felt I'd said my bit, and the rest of the evening went to plan. But what I didn't know until later was that Sir Clive Thompson, who was sitting next to my wife Pat, said to her immediately after my speech, 'The hairs have just risen on the back of my neck.'

Now Pat is my Rock of Gibraltar, but she is also my greatest critic. And the last thing on earth my wife would do is praise me gratuitously. She didn't that night either – and I knew nothing about the President's reaction until much later.

So a few days later, I was changing planes at Copenhagen airport en route for Birmingham from Helsinki, where I had been doing a job for KPMG. My phone rang and a headhunter's voice said: 'I'd like to talk to you about the new Director-General of the CBI'. I thought he was ringing me for a reference on someone else. So I said, 'Who is it going to be?'

And he said, 'We thought you'd put your name forward'. I was truly astounded and I'm pretty sure I said something like, 'But that sort of job goes to clever, grey-suited people from London, and that's not me.' He said, 'Possibly, but we want to make a difference'.

Presumably he knew I wasn't clever, knew I wasn't grey-suited, knew I didn't come from London, but he carried on to explain that the difference the CBI was looking for – a much more 'in your face' kind of Director-General, someone with a connection and a feeling for the grassroots of business and someone who was less cerebral and less of a management consultant than some previous CBI bosses.

In fact my three predecessors, Adair Turner, Howard Davies and John Banham were originally from the world of management consultancy. The CBI was also becoming remote from its membership. What I didn't know was that the incumbent Director-General, Adair Turner, had told Sir Clive Thompson that he wanted to go by the end of the year.

Adair had done a very good job – no doubt about it – but he is a very cerebral man. The CBI wanted a complete change.

What I hadn't known was that while Sir Clive Thompson had been sitting in the Botanical Gardens, listening to his slightly less damp Regional Chairman, headhunters were hard at work looking for a new DG of the CBI.

I asked the headhunter to fax me the job description, and flew back to Birmingham. Pat came to meet me at the airport, with the fax, and on the way home I asked her what she thought about the job. She said, 'It's you'. 'But', I said, 'have you seen the money – it's a third of what I earn now'.

Pat looked straight at me and said, 'Well, I'm up for it if you are', and that was it.

Interviews followed with what they called at the CBI, the 'troika', the three Presidents of the CBI past and present and future – the past president was Sir Colin Marshall, (now Lord Marshall of Knightsbridge), who'd also been Chairman of British Airways, the incumbent President was Sir Clive Thompson, also known

to the City as Mr 20%, because of that huge annual growth figure of his company, Rentokil. And the future President was Iain
Vallance, (now Lord Vallance of Tummell), who had overseen
the privatisation of BT.

Fair to say, I think, that in the interviews my business credentials and views of public policy were given a good run round the
block.

It was with a fair degree of nervousness that I eventually sat
down for a final chat over lunch with Sir Clive. I was thinking
that if I did get the job, our lives would change completely, but
on the other hand, I was happy with what I was doing at KPMG.
Mind you, I had always achieved objectives set before me – so I
knew that I must want it if I was putting myself up for it.

As we were sipping our soup, Sir Clive said, 'I was going to tell
you at the end, but I'll tell you now. You've got the job … Now,
how are we going to do it together?'

'Together' was an important word. It implied the leadership and
confidence that Clive was very good at. At the same time, it was
clear that he and I agreed on what the CBI was. It was above all
an independent-minded membership organisation, which re-
lied upon discretionary subscription income and we needed – I
needed – to take it back to its membership, returning it to its
core business.

Sir Clive also said something else which would come to change the face of the CBI and The Voice of Business in the national agenda, 'If I hear that you are upsetting every politician in town, you are doing your job. I want the CBI in the news and I will support you'.

***

My career at the CBI began on Monday, 4 January 2000. The next Saturday I called all the senior employees in. I got started straight away.

I explained my philosophy; 'We exist on discretionary spend. Our subscriptions come from people, from the smallest to the biggest companies in the land. They don't have to pay us. So we've got to love 'em to bits.'

And I actually wrote it down and posted it on the wall – Love Your Members to Bits. From then on, everything was predicated on 'the customer first'. A lot of people at the CBI found that difficult because up until then they'd led an establishment way of life – protected, comfortable, almost elitist. Both Edge & Ellison and KPMG were members of the CBI, and I had sensed for some time through my involvement that the CBI thought – because they were linking with government – that they were somehow above the members and above the day-to-day concerns of basic business.

I asked the meeting, 'Who is your most important client, who are you trying to please every week?' and one of the CBI directors said, 'the government'. I said, 'That's absolute rubbish. The government are the people whom you are trying to influence – you are a transparently paid lobbyist. It's your members whom you are going to please and you', I repeated, 'are going to love 'em to bits'. In essence it was the same thing that my dad told me when I was eight years old in that shop – the customer comes first, second and third.

When you look at the public sector today, there will be many a person who goes into a department such as I found the CBI in 2000, stuffed full of really good people but living in an organisational DNA where people aren't putting the customer first. They look inward, and think more of their own systems rather than the customer. They will never admit this of course, even to themselves.

So that was the first fundamental change I made. Putting the members first meant going out to see them at every opportunity. I went to a region of England or a devolved nation of the UK every week. I would visit four or five businesses, with a round-table chat at lunchtime with businessmen and women, and often an official dinner with about 200 guests – I would also try to see local politicians and some local media. In six and a half years I must have visited well over a thousand companies.

I had always been fascinated by the working of business ever since those first, rather simplistic rules from my dad's shop, but now I was in the guts of the big stuff, every day.

My twenty years in the commercial Birmingham law firm Edge & Ellison had helped me in so many ways. Their clients were the businesses of the heartland of the nation and, as lawyers, we came to understand them intimately. I joined it as an articled clerk in 1978 and left as senior partner 20 years later. As the firm grew rapidly I became deeply involved in the actual running of the business, making judgements on commercial risk, employing people, sadly having to let some go, attracting new work and always, always putting the client first, second and third.

So, at the CBI, I would get onto the shop floor of a manufacturing facility and shout out loud 'this is where money is made – making things!'. In my first year I got around some 200 companies all very different, but usually with a similar refrain – please, government, leave us alone to get on with what we do best, which is running our business. I saw the strain of deadlines and cash flow, the burden of ridiculous regulation and all the day-to-day worries that come between a business and its suppliers, its customers and its employees. It forged in me a deep respect for their efforts, and I also wanted the politicians and civil servants who imposed the festoons of red tape around these creative risk takers to understand how easy it is to strangle our wealth creators and cut off the very lifeblood of our country.

This different focus – a greater, outward-facing role for the boss of the CBI, was also quite a delicate one. Sir Clive Thompson put it to me like this, 'You've got to walk this tightrope between having access to government and not being in the government's pocket. Independence is vital. But you must also never irritate them to the point where they don't give you access, because the biggest thing you sell to members of the CBI is access to government.'

So, at the CBI, I would get onto the shop floor of a manufacturing facility and shout out loud 'this is where money is made – making things!'

Juggling that independence, the love affair with the members, the devious ways of politics and the demands and opportunities of the media first hit me when our possible entry into the Euro was the big national and business issue, in 2000.

There was a considerable amount of flak flying around about the whole issue, and the government was looking at possibly taking a lot of damage. But Tony Blair was playing a blinder. He was letting the CBI take all the mud being thrown around in the Euro debate.

I could sense him enjoying the fact the CBI was riven over the issue – and that wasn't helped by Adair Turner's earlier CBI survey which had come up with the result that 52% of the members were for it, 15% were against and about a third said they'd like to wait and see. He'd used the survey to say that only a small proportion of members were against it, but that didn't include the 'wait-and-sees', who could have gone either way, and it gave the strong impression that the CBI was in favour of the Euro.

The 15% minority were vociferous and important members. They and many of the 'wait-and-sees' were quite prepared to make this a resignation issue. So much time was devoted to this (and had been for a couple of years), that the government was being let off the hook on major issues for business: from education to transport, from taxation to regulation. I needed to work out a way of protecting the CBI and its membership from being pushed around by politics. One skill I'd brought with me from my lawyer background was the ability to distil down, separate out and prioritise things in simple terms. I can remember my Edge & Ellison managing partner, Gil Hayward, telling me often to focus on what matters and leave the rest, no matter how tempting it may be to get involved in the other stuff.

It was a Friday and I was in one of the regions with Kevin Brown of the *Financial Times*. I'd taken him with me to see how I was changing the CBI. And at the end of that day he interviewed me. We talked about transport, we talked about regulation, we talked about tax and then we talked, inevitably, about the Euro, since every interview at that time with every journalist always covered the Euro.

'Kevin', I said, very matter of fact, ' I have to tell you that, frankly, I'm not getting into this debate. We have a democratically elected government and when *they* make their decision to hold a referendum, I'll go to my members and ask them if they want to say yes or no to the Euro, and then we will have the argument. But until the democratically elected government of the day holds a referendum, I am taking it off the agenda. I want to fight for a better business environment in this country in or out of the Euro, and I'm not going be diverted from that by a government's indecision on one issue.'

On the Monday morning the headline on the front page of the *Financial Times* was, 'CBI Stops Promoting Euro'. I thought, 'who on earth had said that?' – because I didn't give it the importance that others clearly did. I didn't see what I'd said as a shift in policy. Anyone would have thought I'd committed a terrible sin. The balloon really went up. Evidently I'd changed the CBI's policy on the hoof.

But I was simply taking the Euro off the agenda.

So, the media's interest now slowly moved away from the CBI's stance on the Euro. I hadn't intentionally manipulated the media, merely stated a fact. The result was that I could get on with the proper business of the CBI. An important day at the CBI, no matter how naively I'd got there.

But the other important lesson of the Euro affair was how, for me, it underlined Sir Clive Thompson's leadership. In the middle of the row he came in to me privately, and said, 'OK, you've done it. Now how are we going to stand firm together? There are those in the membership who want to join the Euro and who are going to ask "why have you done this without talking to us?"' Although he was a hard taskmaster as a chairman, he was really supportive of me. A CEO can ask for little more. That internal debate continued at the highest level in the CBI, but the most important thing was Thompson's use of the word 'we' – it showed just the support I needed in those ensuing months.

The high level affirmation of what I'd achieved on that day finally happened when a couple of years later I was in the office of Jonathan Powell, Blair's Chief of Staff. In the course of our conversation I asked him whether he and the Prime Minister used to give my predecessors such access and he said, 'God no'.

I asked, 'then, why me?'

'Because we never know what you're going to say next. One day you're supporting us and the next day you're not. We have to stay engaged with you to find out where you are.'

I said, 'Well that might be because one day you do something good for business, the next day you don't. I have no political agenda. I don't want to curry favour any more than I want to annoy you. I'm doing this because this is what business wants, and I know that because I talk to business somewhere in the country every day.'

It was then that I realised that to have stopped the CBI being the sacrificial lamb on the altar of the Euro and to have underlined its independence was one of the best day's work I had ever done.

It also showed me how important a relationship between business and the media is. I know that's hardly a huge insight, but the newspapers, radio and television always have a default setting for business and it's either in the business section towards the back end of the paper, or just before the weather from the broadcasters' point of view. Unless, of course, there's a problem. Journalists love problems, gaffes, sackings, resignations, failures. As do their readers, listeners and viewers. I'm not about to wander into the 'good news' debate because that's a losing argument, but my almost accidental news management of the Euro story showed me its power, and its attention span, which can turn on a sixpence.

It can also bite you in very unexpected places.

Michael Harrison from the *Independent* came to interview me at the CBI, late and wringing wet. There had been no shelter on his station and the train was late – and he was in quite an irritated state. As he took off his coat he said, 'Britain is a bloody banana republic, isn't it?', and I replied, ' I know what you mean. Now sit down, have a cup of tea and take the weight off your feet.' Then he interviewed me about transport, regulation and taxation.

The next day I was going into the BBC to do some early morning radio and the young person who met me at the door and took me up to the studio said: 'Oh, by the way, the first question is: what do you think about the lead story in the *Independent* this morning and what you said about Britain?' To which I replied, 'What have I said about Britain?', and he said, 'That it's a banana republic'.

'I've never said it's a banana republic', I retorted.

'Oh yes, you have.' And there it was in black and white.

Well, I dealt with the question and later, I spoke to Michael Harrison and told him that I'd never said anything about Britain being a banana republic.

His response was, 'But you didn't deny it, did you?'

It was a very good lesson. Journalists are professional people and they are paid to do that sort of thing. And it's no good moaning about it. Accept it and move on, wiser if a little sadder.

One of my first TV interviews was live from my first annual CBI dinner at the Grosvenor Hotel on Park Lane. Always a fabulous affair with the Guest of Honour alternately the Prime Minister and the Chancellor of the Exchequer. As I was standing there on the balcony looking down on the best attended business dinner in London, the producer told me down the line that the first question would be, 'Do you think you've heard anything tonight that makes you think this government's business friendly?'

I was therefore a tad surprised when the first live question was nothing of the sort. Instead I was asked straight away whether or not Britain should join the Euro.

Now I intentionally never had a day's media training at the CBI, because I desperately wanted to be me and not become another trained talking head. There would be a fair few mistakes but I learn quickly.

So I instinctively replied that the Euro was very important, but what I should have been asked on such a night was: have all those business people heard anything that makes them think this government is business friendly?

That was the 'right' answer. It was daunting for a rookie, but business must engage the media and shout its case as never before. We must get business on the news for good reasons; TV producers should be including businessmen and women in programme line-ups for positive stories and not just when there's a fraud or a redundancy situation. The main news channels are important but get onto your local radio station, where you'll find a content-poor producer who will welcome you to talk about local business issues which you will have researched from your local newspaper, and you'll also find an audience which you never knew existed – that's just one example. The quality dailies and Radio 4 are important but so are the tabloids and the lighter radio and TV programmes. Let us get business out to all of society.

I've met other business people who do their best to avoid the media – sometimes because they're apprehensive, but often because they see no immediate return in it.

I say to them, the more you do it, the better you get. Always, always answer the question. That will distinguish you from politicians, and broadcasters will like you for it. By owning and running a business you are a leader in society. Leaders have to stand up and be counted. No matter how uncomfortable you think it is, you've got to do it. And one of the biggest reasons why the CBI changed so much was because of its bigger media profile. Peoples' opinions are set by the media, and fixing Britain is becoming the big story – because the seriousness of the problems we face is now coming into every home. This is no longer about some lay-offs in a factory somewhere else – Britain's malaise is everybody's problem, and the media's agenda will shift towards it. Business *must* be centre stage.

***

But with the high CBI profile came the big game politics. We were now in a space where I was forced to lock horns with Gordon Brown. We needed to stand up to him, or let down the very people who paid our wages and thus lose the CBI's valuable independence.

For a few years, we had a good working relationship and I felt that Labour had done some very good things for the stability of the economy. Whatever else business likes, a firm, predictable economy with no surprises is a very encouraging basis upon which to operate and, most importantly, plan. I would give speeches about the independence which Labour had given to the Bank of England – something the Tories never did – and I'd point out that here was a Labour government that was cutting Capital Gains tax to 10%, again something the Tories hadn't done, and it seemed as though this was a more business-engaged government than the CBI had seen for a long time.

Then came the shock of my CBI life. In the 2002 Budget, Brown increased National Insurance contributions for employers by 1%.

I was dumbfounded.

Many journalists asked me why, if the CBI were so included in government thinking, I hadn't seen this coming? Fair point – I didn't even see it in the tea leaves.

It was totally unexpected. For some reason, and I still don't know why, Gordon Brown had fundamentally changed his attitude to

I was dumbfounded ... Gordon Brown had fundamentally changed his attitude to business.

business; the rise in a tax on creating jobs, not making profits, showed that.

I wonder now if he felt he would become Prime Minister earlier than he eventually did and so he felt that in 2002 he could change course and use some years of good economic performance to support 'borrow and spend' and thus bolster a feel-good factor to take with him into Number 10. He was, of course, made to wait and the borrowing has crippled us. I guess we will never know.

He went for a big tax hike and spent it on an unreformed NHS – and he wasn't going to tell anyone until it happened. I don't think even Blair knew until the Cabinet meeting that morning.

So, it completely wrong footed us. I went on the main evening news bulletins and said 'This is a tax on jobs – it's not a tax on profits. National Insurance for employees is a tax on earnings through wages. National Insurance for employers is simply a tax on the jobs they create. Loss-making businesses also pay National Insurance. He hasn't even tried to reform the public sector. The money should go in *after* reform.'

That night, I was speaking at the British Venture Capitalists' Association's annual dinner at the Grosvenor. As I left and was standing on Park Lane waiting to get a cab, my phone rang. It was Gordon Brown. He wasn't happy. He asked me why I was criticising him. Didn't I know that 'it had to be done'?

In the run up to the 2010 General Election there was a debate again about increasing employers' National Insurance contributions. So many politicians see it as a tax on the bosses. But they couldn't be more wrong. It is a tax on creating employment, period. It should be abolished. Tax profits, not employment.

I said to the Chancellor, 'It didn't *have* to be done. Why didn't you talk to us about another way of raising the money, because there are many other ways of doing it rather than taxing jobs.' I told the Chancellor of the Exchequer that he should not put money into the NHS, without reforming the system.

So he asked me, then, if I would chair a committee to do precisely that, to reform the NHS.

I said I'd give it some thought.

Next day I spoke to the Deputy Director-General of the CBI, John Cridland, a wonderful colleague, my right-hand man, and the person who really ran the organisation. Without John none of the progress at the CBI would have been possible. I am personally delighted he is now Director-General of the CBI, richly deserved and good for our country. He told me not to go anywhere near the Chancellor's offer. Regardless of the 'independence' of the position, I would be going inside the tent. The CBI would lose its essential independence.

That was excellent advice, but that night changed Gordon Brown's attitude to me. I wasn't going to go 'inside'. Which made life rather interesting, since there was no doubt in my mind that Brown ran the country day-to-day. For example, there was to be a skills and business seminar, so Charles Clarke, the then Minister for Education and Patricia Hewitt at the DTI got Chris Humphries at the Chambers of Commerce, George Cox at the Institute of Directors and me together, making the most of the excellent personal relationship between the three of us and our organisations which all do good jobs for different constituencies in different ways – and then in walked Gordon Brown. I wondered what it had to do with him and clearly my wonderings were shared by Clarke and Hewitt. The Chancellor took it all over. He cared, he was informed. Gordon was clearly in charge of policy domestically and Blair, as it were, chaired the country and ran its overseas operations.

Overseas, of course, has always been the challenge for Britain. Not just exporting to other countries, but competing with them as a base for business.

The CBI's chief economist, Ian MacAfferty, had done a fine piece of work which examined our competitive edge. It was October 2003 and the work included an assessment of comparative tax regimes and the international competitiveness of the UK tax structure. One of the examples was Ford, who then made cars both in Britain and Germany. Their concern wasn't about each country's headline rate of tax – because although the German tax rate was higher than Britain's, the local districts in Germany, the Lander, would give them allowances, which made the tax cheques they wrote less there than in the UK. It was the question of the amount of tax paid that influenced their location decisions, not the tax structures.

This was a great piece of work and we wanted to get it out to the media as soon as possible. Usually, out of courtesy to the government, we'd let the relevant department know 24 hours before that we were going to publish something, so that when the journalists called them they would already be informed about what we'd done and they'd be prepared for the journalists' questions.

But we were beginning to notice that as soon as the Treasury got notice of our publication, they'd try to ignore any embargo and start a spoiling action, putting their spin on it – and Gordon Brown or Ed Balls would then say that it was nothing to do with them.

So this time, and I knew this particular report was dynamite as far as the Treasury was concerned, we decided to give it to journalists in time for their Monday editions, but didn't give it to the Treasury until after the Sunday newspapers had been printed.

Gordon Brown rang me on that Sunday morning and asked how this would look for the UK's reputation and urged me not to publish it. I told him that my responsibility was to my membership. If the document was factually wrong I would change it. But if it was simply a matter of his opinion, then I had no intention of not publishing it. I told him that it was also my role as an independent lobbyist.

He undoubtedly respected that and I even sensed a wry smile in his voice when I observed that the way out of this disagreement was for UK business taxes to be more internationally competitive. But while I never once heard the swearing and shouting that others have attributed to him, to say he was angry would be an understatement.

The report was published. The Treasury tried its best to spin against it. The membership was delighted. And a CBI/Treasury stand off began. Meetings between the CBI and the government were cancelled at all sorts of levels. Access was denied. Upwards pressure was applied. It was all very petty but, at the time, very daunting. We stood our ground.

Sir John Egan was CBI President at the time and he was terrific – a pugilist who stood right there, sleeves rolled up, by my side, taking the blows with me. The organisation could not wish for anything more from its chairman.

But out of all that came some good. We'd shown we weren't going to be bullied and after a few days Gordon asked to see me in
private. I accepted his invitation and we had coffee on the balcony
overlooking the garden at Number 11. He realised that the CBI
was not going to yield or compromise its independence, but he
told me that he genuinely wanted to make the UK the best place to
do business in Europe, if not the world. His passion for the country shone through and he suggested regular meetings of just the
two of us to discuss competitiveness and business policy. Charm
offensive? For sure. But of use to a lobbyist? You bet.

> **British business
> is nothing
> abroad unless
> it's globally
> competitive.**

Interestingly, in this very personal meeting, (and in
all other private ones where his guard dropped on
many issues), he never once referred to all the rows
and warfare with Number 10 that were and, at the
end of the former Labour government's 'memoir
fest', remained the talk of the town. With me he was always loyal
to his neighbour in particular and his government in general.

The CBI study which caused it all was very important. British
business is nothing abroad unless it's globally competitive. And
there is some very clever competition out there. Britain finds it
difficult to compete on price, but it can usually more than hold
its own in innovation and adding value.

There is also a marginal X-factor in all this, which is the power
of commercial diplomacy at government level. Our expertise in

this delicate and cunning art of statecraft is legendary. But it had serious failings when it came to exploiting the 'special relationship' that we are supposed to have with the USA.

***

We were very much on the receiving end of it, and co-ordinated exploitation of globalisation is so critical to all our futures. It is so frustrating that we, an open, globally engaged, non-protectionist country give way so often in the face of a protectionist America on one side and fortress Europe on the other.

Our relationship with America was disappointing for UK business given the perception of our shared history. The CBI's Washington office kept noticing that our diplomatic tactics with the US were characterised by the amazing ability of the British government to lie down and have its tummy tickled by the Americans. They legged us over at every opportunity.

And the people *not* to blame were the Americans. They have never seen a special relationship between the USA and the UK (except in the area of intelligence), and they happily allow us to think there is one, to their advantage.

What I could never understand, and still don't, is that Tony Blair had put his entire political career on the line over Iraq. It's the one thing he's remembered for, more than anything else. It completely eclipsed everything else that the man did. And history is still proving me right. But he never used it as leverage for commercial advantage for Britain.

I'm not talking about contracts in Iraq, although it was interesting that some countries put few troops in and got a lot of commercial work out of it. Profiting on the deaths of soldiers and civilians is not and must never be Britain's game.

What I wanted was for the UK to use some of its influence and political capital gained in Washington to deal with America's trading stance, which was hurting Britain in other unrelated areas. For example, America's trade barriers. One time, when Blair was off to Washington, I asked his Chief of Staff, Jonathan Powell, 'can you explain to me why United Airlines are allowed to pick up passengers at Heathrow and put them down in Frankfurt, while British Airways or Virgin aren't allowed to pick up passengers in New York and put them down in Chicago?'

Powell agreed with me that it was, and remains, purely because of American protectionism. I said, 'but given that you are sacrificing your entire political standing upon Bush's Iraq adventure, how about going in and saying, I think you owe us – how about cutting us some slack here?'

Blair didn't even try. The British government simply wouldn't do it. I thought that was amazing and very frustrating.

The reality of our relationship with the US is exposed by the Extradition Act of 2003. It is one of the most imbalanced pieces of legislation ever. Americans are allowed to say to the British judicial system, 'we want him'. No case to be proven, merely an assertion. A law passed, according to government minister after government minister, to counter terrorism and money laundering, was used by the US to extradite British business people on alleged business-related offences, who had been found guilty of nothing according to UK law. Judges were powerless to stop it happening. Their job was to interpret the law of the land as passed by Parliament. As aliens, those extradited are banged up without trial or, sometimes, after huge pressure from the UK government, bailed on draconian conditions. There is no award of defence costs even if they win. Their trials are delayed to extend incarceration or increase cost, and thus put maximum pressure on them to come to the plea-bargain table and settle for a short sentence after a guilty plea rather than risk 30 years in a high security prison. No open prisons for aliens. Would the American judicial system give these people a fair trial? For sure. But, and the 'but' is enormous, the case never gets there because the pressure to settle is so great. Tony Blair's government wilfully and happily sent our country's citizens into that hell when not one word had been uttered, not one piece of evidence produced by way of a trial on the facts of the matter. Magna Carta? Habeas corpus? Innocent until proven guilty? Not when extradition to the home of the brave and the land of the free is concerned!

It is an affront to British justice and to our hard-won freedoms. And Blair just let it happen. It is not a question of whether or not the accused did or did not do something wrong. Where was the trial? The public establishment of the facts? The open fairness of balance between prosecution and defence?

America would never allow Britain to extradite in similar fashion the other way. But they get away with it. I have never understood why we are so supine. And don't blame the US. If you lie down and give all the signals that you are happy to be screwed over, then don't blame the person for screwing you over. It's the fault of the person lying down when they can do something about it and we certainly could have stopped this one.

If you lie down and give all the signals that you are happy to be screwed over, then don't blame the person for screwing you over.

***

But, domestically, Blair did at least do something which will be fundamental to our economic and social survival and that was to get nuclear power back onto the agenda. Where it still remains today, although it will still be for the private sector to finance it. But back in 2003 the Energy White Paper, under the Minister of State for, *inter alia*, Energy, Patricia Hewitt, had little about nuclear power in it, apart from this vague reference:

The existing fleet of nuclear power stations will almost all have reached the end of their working lives. If new nuclear power plant [sic] is needed to help meet the UK's carbon aims, this will be subject to later decision.

They had ducked it! Put it in the too-difficult box. Another sop, just like the fox-hunting issue, to the left wing of the party! But we all knew that there would eventually be an energy crisis which 'sustainable' sources simply could not meet.

The CBI was agitating for nuclear power to be brought into the centre of government policy. Our calculation was that the lights would go out in 15 years' time if it wasn't adopted as a major part of our energy resources. We campaigned for a mix of clean coal, gas, wind, tidal … and nuclear. Not only from a 'clean' point of view but also from concerns about security of supply. We at the CBI were frustrated that the anti-nuclear constituency tried to block attempts to protect our country, and yet acquiesced to electricity being generated mostly by nuclear power 27 miles across the Straits of Dover and exported through the Interconnector to us. Some 80% of French electricity is nuclear-generated and no one here says a word!

Blair deserves credit for forcing nuclear energy back onto the agenda and, as it happened, pressing on with it during a rather entertaining show at the CBI National Conference. That year, 2005, it was held in Islington and, entirely appropriately in that

champagne socialist London borough, two Green-
peace protesters had climbed up to the rafters of the
Conference Hall. Their 'Representative on Earth'
said to me that unless he could read out a prepared
statement before the Prime Minister spoke then the
men in the rafters would peacefully but very nois-

Blair deserves credit for forcing nuclear energy back onto the agenda.

ily disrupt the speech. Unacceptable! I told him that all speech-
makers at CBI Conferences took questions afterwards so I would
ensure he got the first question. He refused, saying he was 'not
mandated' to agree to any deviation from what he had been ordered to achieve.

Tony Blair was sitting in the Green Room waiting to go on. His
aides were warning him that the delay meant his diary for the
rest of the morning and the whole day was backing up. I was full
of admiration for him when he said: 'I don't care if I wait here all
day, I am delivering this speech.' Armed with this resilient example we found a nearby room that the girders from which the
protesters were hanging didn't reach. There were no chairs and
only a makeshift sound system. I put it openly to the Conference (by now live on the *BBC News* channel) what the situation
was and what both the protesters had said and what our PM had
insisted upon, and our suggested solution. So we all moved into
this small room where I announced (to a gathering including, as
at every CBI Conference, a fair share of overseas diplomats and
business people) that our country had a tradition of allowing
our democratically elected leaders to speak and be questioned

(whether we agreed with them or not) and no demonstrator was going to stop that. The CBI members and the press crammed in, standing up to listen to a PM on top form. He announced the government's decision to put nuclear firmly back on the agenda. The CBI lobbying efforts had delivered. And the rafter-dwellers? Their confused earthling asked me as we all moved out: 'What about them?', pointing to the girders above the hall. 'Not my problem' I replied, quietly thanking a Prime Minister with guts and a CBI membership which didn't stand on ceremony. I think the protesters were brought down by the police some hours later.

That important energy issue had been pushed front of house, where it has remained ever since.

***

Now you would have thought, as the CBI was getting its higher profile that we would be fundamentally opposed to much of what the unions stood for. But I found that there were often matters which united us. I actually got on with the successive General Secretaries of the Trades Union Congress, John Monks (now Lord Monks) and then Brendan Barber.

We would however disagree fundamentally on certain things, like the Working Time Directive. Fixing Britain means not allowing the European Union to impose legislation that eventually sends people to prison for working more than 48 hours a week, on member countries that want to be internationally competitive. China must think it's their birthday! No one should be made to work more than 48 hours a week if they don't want to, but if there are no health and safety issues, why shouldn't people who want to earn more for themselves and their families be free to do so?

When Alan Johnson became Secretary of State for Trade and Industry, I asked him in private, whether or not he and I were going to have a row over the Working Time Directive, which Brussels was trying hard to impose on us. Quite apart from the fact it would hurt the competitiveness of business, I just believe in the freedom of the individual to work if he or she wants to. Alan Johnson told me that he worked for some years as a postman and the only way he could afford a holiday for his kids every year, was to work some overtime. 'So', he said, ' you'll have no problem with me'. Refreshing, to the point, and spot on!

But some of the work that unions do in skilling and helping people improve is first class.

I envisage a lad at work, perhaps in his early thirties. He might have a rudimentary skill but what he does now is done in China, so he needs to skill up. He doesn't trust college, because he had a horrible school life. He doesn't trust his boss, the company he works for. But he does trust his union. Which gives the unions a unique role. They can help train and skill these people in so many walks of life, and the result is often a win–win–win. The country benefits from enhanced productivity, the individual improves in so many ways and the union is – through constructive help not destructively-motivated militancy – relevant to the largest social issue for Britain in the twenty-first century.

Some of the work that unions do in skilling and helping people improve is first class. Another time, when Stephen Byers was the Secretary of State at the Department of Trade and Industry, he rang me up one day and said that he'd be at a Labour Party policy think-tank that weekend, and he asked me if I could tell him the one thing that business wanted more than anything else in that particular year.

I said, 'Sure – abolish the Climate Change Levy'. Byers said, 'That's exactly what Brendan Barber's just said.'

'Well in that case, it's probably right,' I replied. But nothing changes. Our EU rivals watched as we unilaterally sacrificed our competitiveness, as I said at the time, on 'the altar of green credentials'. Global issues like climate change only work on the win–win basis of maintaining international competitiveness *and* cleaning up the planet if every country does it.

But while the unions and the CBI agreed about some fundamental things which would have improved Britain's lot hugely, the politicians were very disappointing.

Forty years ago those unions would have bestrode the fine car-
pets of Downing Street with a special swagger, especially with a
Labour government, but most voters who gave Tony Blair their
endorsement in 1997 must have hoped that the traditional link
between the brothers and Labour had been severed, or at least
diluted, by the 'New' soubriquet of the metropolitan class behind this latest incarnation of the Labour Party. But not so.

The private and public sectors had, for some years, been working
together on big building projects like schools, roads and hospitals, through either Private Public Partnership (PPP) or the
Private Finance Initiative (PFI). The Prime Minister announced
there were going to be combined discussions with government,
the CBI and the unions about how we could make the introduction of the private sector into the public sector more effective
and more efficient.

There were high hopes for this, but then in the newspapers the
next morning was a picture of two or three union leaders going
in to have private conversations with Number 10 and Number 11
about exactly this subject. We hadn't been invited.

I issued a statement saying this was a Labour government that
had clearly not changed its spots, and that there was a doorway
into Downing Street labelled 'unions only'. I observed that the
unions had bought the Labour government through its enormous political donations and this was payback time. Indeed,

the government even went on to announce a grant of ten million pounds of taxpayers' money to the trades unions to 'help them modernise'. What other vested interest or lobby group would get that? And from the taxes of everyone – taxpayers' money specifically helping the funders of the political party in government.

Douglas Alexander, who was a junior minister at the time, rang me, asking if I'd have a chat with him, because I was clearly annoyed.

I went in with one of my advisers and met Douglas Alexander with his adviser, in his office. He asked why I was cross about this and I told him that I'd understood both sides, unions and the CBI, were going to get involved, jointly, and yet it looked as if the agenda was being set in discussions that only included the unions. It was clear to me that the exercise was not about getting the private sector involved. The whole thing was just superficial, constructed to calm down the anti-PPP, anti-PFI unions.

The minister gave a sort of a 'Hmmph!', and without a word, got up and strode out of his own office.

His adviser gathered up all the files, and said 'Errr um' and followed him out. Which left my advisor and me sitting in the minister's office wondering what we ought to do next! There we were in the office of a Minister of the Crown, on our own. And presumably, Douglas Alexander was sitting somewhere else, down the corridor thinking, 'Now what do I do? I've just walked out of my own office!'

We quietly slipped away and in the afternoon I got a call from Number 10 saying that they'd heard there had been a bit of a problem that morning. I had said nothing to anybody, so clearly Douglas Alexander had spoken to someone about it.

I was always surprised at how much credence New Labour gave to the unions specifically as the representatives of the employed in the country.

Number 10 said it was a very emotional subject and that everybody was under huge pressure, and that they were sorry. I said there was no need to apologise, and merely observed if you're going to go off in a huff then don't do it out of your own office, because there's nowhere to go! I rather felt the same about New Labour's initiative.

I was always surprised at how much credence New Labour gave to the unions specifically as the representatives of the employed in the country. By the middle of the first decade of the twenty-first century, unions represented some 12% of the private sector workforce in Britain and only 52% of those employed in the public sector. And yet they were constantly put up by government and media alike as representative of employed Britain. With the restructuring of the economy to a skilled, flexible position and an increasing number of employers from overseas who were attracted by the most flexible labour market in Europe, I asked what place had organisations that went on strike over changes in pension arrangements for those who weren't even employed by the business, or took time off work to protest, as a union not individuals, over a war in a foreign land. Important, of course, but not exactly a workplace issue. I often asked publicly what the unions were doing to get the unemployed into work by the stimulation of a skilled, flexible labour market rather than constantly fighting yesterday's battles. And yet minister after minister, journalist after journalist, would talk of 'the CBI and the unions' as confrontational and traditional bedfellows with status similar to that of the statutorily recognised social partners that similar organisations held across the Channel. Surely 10% unemployment in major EU economies in good times ought to consign such statism to the dustbin of the last century.

And in their rush into power, New Labour signed up to some very destructive governance in those heady days. One was European workplace legislation.

Brown wanted a joint working party formed of unions and the CBI to come up with ideas on how to improve productivity in Britain. But we were not to be allowed to discuss European workplace regulation, which was the real issue.

We, as usual, did most of the work but, surprise, surprise, we agreed on the basics – skills, capital investment, better middle management, helping exports, better transport, less ideological environmental legislation. All the usual good stuff. It seemed, though, a fairly pointless exercise, because we, as I said, weren't allowed to discuss the productivity-destroying EU workplace regulations which Blair, after years of Conservative opposition, had signed up to by adopting the Social Chapter at a stroke in 1997.

One day, we were in Number 10 for a working breakfast with the Prime Minister and I told him that one of business's great problems was the Agency Temps Directive. Temporary staff have been crucial to the flexibility of business, but this directive now makes them subject to all the workplace redundancy, sick leave, employment tribunals and other regulations which apply to full time staff.

The PM got the point and asked who on earth had brought all that to the table? It was left to Blair's Chief of Staff, Jonathan Powell, to tell the Prime Minister that it was, in fact, Anthony Blair himself – when he had signed up to the EU's Social Chapter the moment he came into power in 1997.

It was one small example of a politician who had no understanding of the commercial consequences of what he was doing, and how his ignorance of business had a depressing effect on the creation of tax-generating wealth and jobs in our country.

***

With the wealth of the exporting part of our country very much on my mind, I'd made a pledge that I would try to get to an overseas market every month. In the end I landed in 70 different countries in the six and a half years at the CBI. Our diplomats overseas welcomed the visits and were fantastically cooperative. I was not a visiting government minister or official, and I could say things in speeches that ministers or ambassadors couldn't say, although they would have loved to!

So often, ambassadors who wanted to get that message across used to say to me that a minister could never say that, and they were happy to use me as a sort of heavyweight catalyst with obvious business credentials.

I've also been abroad with unions and government officials with whom I'd quarrel at home. But once you leave these shores, you're all batting on the same wicket. Of course when you come home, you renew hostilities, or 'constructive engagement' depending on who's put a spin on it first! And if we are going to fix Britain, this issue is extremely important. In the next couple of years there are going to be some huge rows at home. If we are really going to maintain and cultivate Brand Britain overseas, those rows should stay at home, behind closed doors. I often disagreed with Tony Woodley of the Unite Union but we attended a conference on manufacturing together in Shanghai. He was excellent at batting for Britain overseas, even when I could tell he would have loved to have 'had a go'.

At the CBI we also campaigned that when those overseas investors whom we'd been cultivating abroad came over here, there
was actually somewhere good to land.

Domestically, we must get our goods to market, our people to
work – which means airports that work, ports that work, roads
that work, and railways that work. But this Coalition government has already said that there will be no third runway at Heathrow – a blow for the CBI's ceaseless campaign to expand a vital
cog in our wheel of international competiveness. I'm marginally
encouraged to hear the Prime Minister and the Foreign Secretary talking about commercial diplomacy, and the projection of
our power overseas to help build business. Lovely words, nicely
crafted – and David Cameron's early visits to India and China,
accompanied by legions of businessmen and women, shows he
'gets it' – but building business in export markets means global
travel. Global travel means aircraft.

You don't need aircraft to get round Britain. I fully understand
that. You don't need aircraft to get to various parts of northern
Europe. I also understand that.

But, if you are going to fly westwards or you are going to fly east-
wards, where are you going to fly from? And if we are going to
generate more and more export activity and inward investment,
we are clearly going to travel more and more.

But with Heathrow full, and Gatwick and Stansted straining – and remember the latter two 'London' airports are being constrained by government diktat as well – how are we going to accommodate the extra traffic?

Those who believe that passengers can be shuttled to Schipol or Charles de Gaulle or Frankfurt are badly, and sadly for UK growth, wrong. The moment you do that, the headquarters of companies will move, simply because they'll go to wherever they can easily get off a plane and go to work. International transfers won't even touch Britain.

Our unrivalled position as *the* place to do business in Europe will diminish rapidly. To solve our problems we need to trade and stimulate flows of capital and people. Successful, efficient airports in the South-East are essential. And sadly when the current government realises that it will, frankly, be too late.

***

Other travellers, our immigrants, though, do more than just touch Britain. I decided to take the CBI into the rather uncomfortable territory of immigration.

I was advised that it would be pretty dangerous, but I wrote articles about it, I made speeches about it and I did so without fear or favour.

I said that what we need in Britain is people from other lands who will speak English, bring a skill, have a job, make themselves wealthier and pay some tax. They are more than welcome in our country.

But if they won't speak English and they won't work and they won't bring a skill then, frankly, this great wonderful democracy of ours that has freedom of speech, and freedom of assembly and freedom of worship, has other freedoms: you are free to leave and you are free not to come. The great experiment to create multicultural Britain has failed. An ethnically integrated Britain can be a huge success. I look forward to the day when a Brit who just happens to have a different coloured skin to me becomes my Prime Minister.

... what we need in Britain is people from other lands who will speak English, bring a skill, have a job, make themselves wealthier and pay some tax. They are more than welcome in our country.

In the past when local authorities or central government have allowed immigrants to come in with their families, and go to the top of the housing list, you can understand why the BNP can fish in very fertile waters. But don't blame the immigrant. Blame British governments and local authorities of all parties over many years who've said, 'it doesn't matter, just come on in'.

In 2006 I made a television programme about immigrant labour. In Peterhead in Scotland, when the fishing fleet came in and landed the fish, the people who actually took the fish off the boat very early in the morning and stacked it up in the cold houses for auction were all Poles. The man who ran them said he'd offered the jobs to young Scots in a place with the highest incidence of youth unemployment in Britain.

He told me that not enough locals had applied and that those that did worked for two or three days, then never came again. So he put an advert in a newspaper in Warsaw and he got more applicants than he could ever deal with; hard workers who always turned up on time. The pay was just above the minimum wage. Two of them were soon promoted and began to manage the others.

I went into a pub near the docks at lunchtime and talked to the Scots lads who were on the dole. I asked them why they were on benefit and they said because all the Poles had taken their jobs. I remarked that they'd been offered the jobs but turned them down. They said that they didn't want to do all that hard work for that sort of money.

They were of course in the pub, drinking. Not *wanting* to work. Of course, the Poles will eventually go home. I wonder what will happen to those jobs then? And what will become of our Scottish fishing fleet?

***

By 2005, I began to feel as if it was time for me to move on.

The Director-General's term at the CBI lasts five years. By that time I'd been working with another President – Sir John Egan, who had been Chief Executive at Jaguar and BAA – who was wonderfully combative and understood business completely. He had fought the unions at Jaguar – had built the company up and floated it on the stock exchange.

The CBI membership were saying that they would like me to stay on. I was very wary of overstaying my welcome – I'd seen business and political leaders do that with unhappy consequences. But the whole thing was going rather well.

The membership was higher than ever, we had internationalised the organisation with offices in Brussels, Beijing and Washington and we'd positioned the CBI where it should be, as the influential, non-party-political Voice of Business.

There was another, important issue. It was 2005: general election year. We were also championing an Olympic bid, the UK held the Presidency of Europe for the first six months and we were chairing the G8 for the whole year. I thought it was better to have an experienced Director-General that year than a brand new one. Plus there was a new president as well at the CBI, who was Sir John Sunderland, the Chairman of Cadbury's, a businessman with whose values and principles I found great common cause. He was a man with considered style, of great common sense, calm and so supportive. He was chairman of the living

... business is the only part of society that generates wealth, and the only part of society that generates jobs and taxation. embodiment of socially inclusive wealth creation, that great British company (alas no more) Cadbury PLC. Incidentally, I often wonder if the Americans would have allowed Cadbury to acquire Kraft in the way we just sat back and watched one of our icons be swallowed up. Level playing field? I don't think so. He was also inspirational on the subject of globalisation which was a passion of mine – so it seemed sensible to stay on for a couple of years until, before the end of 2006, they'd found my successor.

And then there was the general election. Now the CBI had never previously got involved and it had kept its collective head down for the four weeks of hustings.

I had put my toe in the water of publicity in the 2001 campaign, but this time we developed a proper Manifesto for Business. We would say that business is the only part of society that generates wealth, and the only part of society that generates jobs and taxation. That was then, and this truth is just as relevant now.

If we're going to fix Britain, every journalist, every environmentalist, every educationalist, every trades unionist and every politician in the land needs to understand that completely. If you don't have a successful business sector, you have no taxation, no sustainable employment. Period. And they don't seem to get it.

So, in 2006, I left the CBI. I was born into business and business had given me the opportunities of a lifetime. I will always owe the CBI for teaching me, affording me opportunities I would only have dreamed about, deepening my pride in our country, enabling me to develop my understanding of public policy and politics. Above all, it allowed me to work with and for some of the best people in the country, both those in the organisation and those we represented, the businesses of Britain.

I had learnt something rather important too – that business is essentially honest in its endeavours – or at least transparent in what it strives to do, which is to make money. Of course there are some dishonest businessmen and women. They merely re-flect society, in the same way that there are dishonest teachers, conservationists, police officers, doctors and, dare I say it, jour-nalists and civil servants. But what had struck me was the basic dishonesty of the political driver. Politics is, as one former Tory Prime Minister said, about the acquisition, maintenance and use of power.

Whatever politicians say to the contrary, their number one driv-er is survival and promotion. Few admit it of course. Admitted-ly, and to their credit, there's many a Liberal Democrat minister who, over the past few months, has clearly put the country first. But business is there, openly – and hopefully on a socially in-clusive basis – to make a profit. Usually the majority of society benefits hugely but at least we all know what drives it on.

CHAPTER 3

THE GLOBE-TROTTING GOAT – TETHERED BY WESTMINSTER AND WHITEHALL

I was once again face to face with Gordon Brown – a man who'd been often supportive, and often less than helpful in his dealings with British business. Sometimes he appeared as if he understood what business needed and then, on other occasions, he was so wide of the mark that I'd often wondered how such a clever man could get it all so wrong.

We were meeting at his request inside Number 10 on one of the last days of June 2007, 24 hours after Brown had become Prime Minister.

I was pursuing what I hoped would be a profitable, plural career, a year after leaving the CBI.

When he was still Chancellor, and I had left the CBI, I had accepted Brown's invitation to be the part-time, unpaid United Kingdom Skills Envoy. He had introduced an initiative called 'Train to Gain', an excellent idea.

Businesses would work with local colleges on Level 1 and Level 2 standards of training – getting their employees to be able to read, write and count and operate a computer. I'd found some dreadful examples of the lack of basic skills in the workforce, and my job was to give oxygen to solving this problem and getting employers signed up to the plan. At the heart of it was a three-way commitment: the employer allowed some time off for training to take place, the employee adding some of his or her free time to that. The government paid for the training. First in the private sector, and then onto the public sector where the NHS and local authorities were the two largest employers of unskilled people in the country. This was something that I really cared about. I set about it with messianic zeal and it seemed to be going quite well.

I went to see Brown, at his request, on that Wednesday morning, fully expecting him to ask for a progress report on my UK Skills Envoy work and I hoped he would expand its brief. I couldn't have been more wrong and rarely have I been so surprised, shocked actually, as I was that day. He was very businesslike as usual, but his renewed sense of purpose, of reforming zeal, of freshness, was palpable. It was as if he had been set free. He explained how he wanted to get some experienced non-politicians into government where their specific skills could be brought to bear for a limited period to the benefit of the country. A new way of delivering in key areas. He then started to talk to me about the promotion of overseas trade and inward investment.

He said that I'd been complaining for years that politicians had never given it the true clout that it deserved and that governments had never addressed it properly.

He was right – it had regularly enraged me that, when I was at the CBI, we'd been setting out on a trade mission and then the minister had to cancel because there was a vote in the House of Commons or some other matter deemed of greater importance in the bubble that is Westminster. So a crucial trade deal, which could have created jobs in Britain, was often hampered because a minister had to vote for something like the fox-hunting bill; or our goodwill in an important overseas market was diminished by the fear a junior minister had of falling out of favour with 'the centre'.

Now I'd had my problems with Brown in the past, but I'll give him credit for the next bit. He said he wanted 'to change forever the way the government did trade and investment'. The minister should have the confidence of the business community and not be a typical politician in one particular cycle of his career, hopeful of moving on to something else as soon as possible in order to stay in the seat of power.

The Prime Minister of just one day looked at me and said, 'so here's your chance. Let's reform the way we do it. Let's change what we do.' He said he was going to try a big experiment to bring established experts into four areas at ministerial level. In Health there would be Ara Darzi, an eminent surgeon. Security would have the former First Sea Lord, Alan West. Brown proposed Mark Malloch-Brown from the United Nations would be at the Foreign Office, and I would be Minister of State for Trade and Investment. He stressed that this was not going to be the beginning of a career. These were not Cabinet positions. We were to do specific jobs for the country, not politics.

Just as I was starting to establish myself in business again after my years at the CBI, here was Gordon Brown asking that I give up everything that I was doing – all my money-earning – and give some time to the country. It was, I suppose, my National Service. Corporal Jones was once again enrolled in UK PLC, but this time with a very different twist.

In our swift conversation, I had not only the prospect of becoming Minister of State for Trade and Investment, but, because

I had to be in Parliament to be a minister under our current system, I would be going to the House of Lords.

If I agreed to do the job, this lad from a shop in Alvechurch would become Baron Jones of Birmingham.

The new Prime Minister asked me if I would like to ring Pat – I thought I'd like to ring my bank manager, to be honest! I told him I'd call with my thoughts. But even then I knew I was going to do it.

I was in Newcastle that evening pursuing my burgeoning speaking career. I have never had any trouble sleeping, even through some of those personal crises that we all suffer. Indeed I have always enjoyed just six solid hours' sleep a night as one of the keys to a full life. But the enormity of this decision – to abandon my new career plans and walk into a high level government role – kept me awake. Apart from changes to my lifestyle, it would mean yet another life for Pat in the goldfish bowl, more days apart from her and a serious decline in our financial circumstances.

In the morning I called the Cabinet Secretary, Sir Gus O'Donnell. An exemplar among Whitehall's civil servants, he was John Major's press secretary twenty years ago and is widely recognised as one of the most talented civil servants for decades.

Indeed, the country has much to be grateful for, in that Sir Gus was in charge of the successful process in May 2010 when an inconclusive General Election result threatened a constitutional crisis. He's a class act.

I said to him that I would accept and noted that Gordon had asked me to do it for a year, but I felt it should be a for a longer period than that. Everyone expected a general election sooner rather than later.

But I had one important condition. I told Gus that I would not join the Labour Party. He said that it would be a real problem, and asked me if that would be a deal breaker – the line over which I would not tread. I said, yes it would be, it was the 'stopper' as I put it. I added to the point by saying that if Gordon really understood business and really understood the implications of how he said he wanted me to fulfil the task of promoting inward investment and linking in with the business community trading overseas, I would do a much better job if I were not linked to a political party. The role should be seen by one and all as non-party political. I was not there to be a cheer-leader for Labour, nor anti-Tory or Liberal Democrat but for UK PLC.

Gus came back to me a few hours later and said that it would be fine. And to the best of my knowledge I

And to the best of my knowledge I am the only government minister the country has ever had that has openly not belonged to the party of the government of the day.

am the only government minister the country has ever had that has openly not belonged to the party of the government of the day.

***

It was late Thursday afternoon, and a government car picked me up from King's Cross station and took me to Whitehall.

Sir Gus O'Donnell met me and took me into a lovely, high windowed, wood panelled boardroom.

In walked my 'Sir Humphrey', the Permanent Secretary at the recently rebranded Department for Business, Enterprise and Regulatory Reform (BERR), Sir Brian Bender. I'd known him from my days at the CBI – he shook my hand and said that first he should offer his congratulations. He told me that this was the first time that 'Business' had been used in the title of the department of government that looked after business. But he also told me that he thought I was mad and that I wouldn't fit in at all.

When I said that I was in here to bring about a change in the way things got done at Trade and Investment, he just smiled.

There was a bigger smile, I think, on the next newcomer's face. Sir Brian and I were sitting behind one of the two enormous doors which led into the room. We couldn't see who this person was, but she was clearly a new minister, a time-serving politician on the threshold of her career, and she was getting a conducted tour from her permanent secretary. He was telling her that this room would be one of hers. She sounded completely overjoyed by the surroundings and she said to her new civil servant that this was what she'd worked for. Here she was with the first smell of power. A career politician to whom the nice big office, the car and the obliging officials were the rewards of her efforts. She had no idea (and probably still doesn't) we were there behind the door. I remember thinking right then just where the people who had voted for her stood in her order of priorities.

I wondered which of our approaches was the more honest. Hers because she told her constituents that she cared for them but was also enjoying the trappings of power? Or mine, because I would be trying to trade Britain into a better place, but I was, at the same time, an unelected minister of state with a privileged seat in the Lords, who had never been through the democratic process?

That evening, the Lord Jones-to-be resumed for one last time his normal job and travelled away from Whitehall, to Oxfordshire, where the next morning I would be speaking at a breakfast raising money for charity.

I arrived in my hotel room, and turned on the TV to watch *Newsnight*. Much to my surprise I heard 'Digby Jones' mentioned and I learned that I had been made Minister of State for Trade and Investment in Gordon Brown's new government.

When I had left Whitehall earlier that evening, I'd been told that all this was going to be announced the next day at a news conference which I would attend and that a statement agreed by me in advance would be issued.

I should have known better. That was Labour's way. Spin before the announcement, push out a selected version of the facts. How familiar that was!

But there was worse. Sitting next to the *Newsnight* presenter was some political correspondent who opined that how interesting it was that Digby Jones was not only taking up this new job, was not only accepting a peerage, but was also going to vote with and be a member of the Labour Party.

That was so wrong and so damaging, not just to me personally, but to everyone who had always seen me as the independent voice for business. I needed to correct it immediately.

I had no press office to help me in the normal way. I felt very alone and vulnerable. I called the Downing Street switchboard there and then. During my CBI years I'd always had a rapport with the Number 10 operators, and they were like the mother ship. They are the one contact point that can find anybody. I knew I was pushing my luck, but I asked the lady who answered if she had a number for the BBC, because I needed to get through to the *Newsnight* programme urgently before it went off air. The operator, bless her, said that she could do better than that and could put me through to the actual programme production desk. From a bedroom in rural Oxfordshire, I spoke to the BBC *Newsnight* producer directly; he must have fed it straight into the presenter's earpiece because in a matter of seconds he was saying that Digby Jones had just called in to say that he was not in fact joining the Labour Party.

It could have been damaging spin, but I managed to nip it in the bud. A completely lucky break – and it made me realise how important it is to be a 'do as you would be done by' kind of person. I've always made it a personal rule to respect *everybody's* position in an organisation. Every employee counts– I've always thought they are my equal, we are just doing different jobs. That night my years of treating the switchboard operators as I would like to be treated paid off, and how!

That last minute intervention had worked, but at the back of my mind was a nagging thought. Very much along the lines of 'Oh my God, what have I done?'

The next morning, after I'd given my speech at the charity event, I rang my new Permanent Secretary Sir Brian Bender, and asked him what I should do when I got back to London. He told me to go to our flat in Marylebone and wait for the call to come down to the offices of BERR in Victoria Street.

The call never came. After four or five hours of hanging around (I have a pathological dislike for hanging around for five unproductive minutes, let alone five hours!), I rang my new office and asked to speak to Bender, to which came the reply from his staff that they were all 'very, very busy'. I wanted to get on with my new job, go to the offices of UKTI, the organisation within BERR for which I had responsibility, to meet the people and start work. It is vital at times of big change that leaders get down onto 'the shop floor' immediately, communicating, being seen, saying hi. But man-management has never been the machinery of government's strong suit. I wanted to start making a difference now! The office asked me to wait, but it simply wasn't my way of doing business. I could see that process was winning over outcomes. So I said that I was going home to Warwickshire and frankly, as far as I was concerned, it could all wait until Monday.

That Friday evening, I finally had some official contact about the new job, not from my new department but from the boss himself. Gordon Brown called and welcomed me to the new role and even apologised for not calling before! I was impressed how the country's Prime Minister could find the time to talk to very low pond life like me when senior civil servants clearly could not. We talked about my not joining the Party, and he asked if I would still vote with the Labour government. I said that what I would do is never embarrass him and would never vote against the government in the Lords. If I were available to vote, I said I would vote with the Labour whip.

I told him that I planned to revolutionise the way the Trade job was done and I would be out of the country most of the time, so problems about my voting would rarely arise. The Prime Minister thought that was a good idea.

Many people said that I was simply avoiding the issue, and they were absolutely right. My job was to go abroad as a Minister of the Crown and sell Brand Britain, stimulating trade and attracting inward investment, not going into the House of Lords as lobby fodder to vote. This was precisely the change that was needed, but I could sense the trouble brewing.

I'd become what Whitehall would begin to call, with its habitual wish for acronyms, a GOAT. Brown decided to bring four outsiders at ministerial level into what he thought were crucial areas of government.

He was creating a Government Of All the Talents, hence the 'GOAT' label. But if Whitehall thought that, in me, they were about to have some stereotypical minister they were very much mistaken.

My office was, quite seriously, a designated broom cupboard down the corridor from the Secretary of State for Business, John Hutton. But the Offices of UK Trade and Investment, my department within BERR, were half a mile away further down Victoria Street in Kingsgate House. My office had been created out of a broom cupboard (with my PA sitting in the corridor outside) because the civil servants in the Broom Cupboard Location and Resettlement Department had thought that I wanted to be close to the real power of the Business Department, the Secretary of State. A perfectly rational and normal assumption because junior ministers on the first rung of a hopefully long and illustrious ministerial career would want to be close to the power source, where the career-enhancing deals and decisions were made.

But what I hadn't expected was the omnipotent suffocation of the Parliamentary process and the obligatory emasculation of original thought and initiative.

But I wasn't one of them. I knew I would be spending very little time in the office and when I did, I wanted to be with my team at UKTI. So I became the first minister of that department who decided to base himself away from the Tower of Power at 1

Victoria Street. My new colleagues at UKTI were delighted, and so, I guess, were the officials up the road at BERR!

But they were all mystified, though, when after a few weeks they saw a piece of paper on the front of my desk which had the following written on it… 'oooosssshhhhwwwrrrcccchhh'.

They asked what it was. I said it was the most common sound (through clenched teeth and pursed lips) that I heard when I wanted to do something differently. That sound would, invariably, be followed by 'I wouldn't do that, Minister', or 'very brave, Minister' – the entire place was risk averse, so that the most common advice all too readily accepted by career politicians not wanting to blot their ministerial-progress copybook was to do nothing. And I never managed to change that.

But what I hadn't expected was the omnipotent suffocation by process and the obligatory emasculation of original thought and initiative. The governmental machine demanded complete obedience in a way which anyone outside the Westminster bubble wouldn't have believed, and it distanced the parties and politicians from the real world and the real voters. In amongst the obduracy and the 'not invented here' approach of Whitehall I found the ministers themselves a delight to work with – helpful, decent, hard-working – indeed, overworked and often overtired people doing their best.

John Hutton, Pat McFadden and Lord Willy Bach at BERR in their welcoming engagement; David Milliband in his personal attention and clear understanding of the importance of projecting this country's influence around the world through international business and commercial diplomacy; the cheerful and tolerant help and advice of Cathy Ashton and Jan Royall in the Lords. They all understood what the Prime Minister was trying to achieve with the GOATS and supported me at every turn and with every problem.

We understood one another, and important stands had to be made in the face of the bureaucratic nonsense that governed in Whitehall, and the diary of Parliamentary business which 'the system' employed to overrule a sense of the new priorities. The benefit to this country of international trade missions or a speech in a region of the country had been weakened in the past by some civil servant waving a diary in the ministerial face to make sure that he or she wasn't missing some vote or other, with no thought to the relevant importance of the real job the minister was employed by the taxpayer to do.

***

While I was irritated by the constant need to get permission simply to do my job, I was shocked at the herd-like behaviour of many of my fellow Parliamentarians in both Houses.

Cabinet may decide policies but ministers often lack the skills to be able to deliver them from a basis of experience and understanding. When the Commons Division Bell sounds, I've seen MPs rushing out of their offices or meeting rooms, out of bars and restaurants and into the Lobby. Often they don't know what the vote is specifically about. They would be told how to vote by the Party Whips. They hadn't of course understood one of the prime functions of the House of Commons, which is the debate and argument, and they had voted in complete ignorance of the real issue – and this is democracy?

The electorate might think that politics is about caring for, or fighting for, a cause and that's what they are encouraged to believe; I know that there are some MPs who give the specific lie to my generalisation. But politics is really about the acquisition, maintenance and use of power. Any implementation of independent thinking away from the party line is usually fatal to a career.

Unfortunately, within such machinations is a rich seam of inability. Cabinet may decide policies but ministers often lack the skills to be able to deliver them from a basis of experience and understanding. At 'Questions' in either House, the average minister would have his or her answers prepared by a whole posse of civil servants – good and diligent people, but the average minister needed to be prepped because he or she will rarely know enough about the subject. And, in any case, a Minister for

Transport who after a few months moves to Health and then onto the Treasury in fairly short order is not going to have the time to master a brief – which means that government decisions lack the specific informational (as opposed to the political) expertise that they deserve and to which the voters are entitled.

I also wondered whether the voters would expect the United Kingdom Trade Minister's official car to be made in Japan. I had been assigned a Honda hybrid *not* made at the Honda plant in Swindon in the UK. I told my bureaucrats that since we were all paid by the taxpayer, many of whom worked in Britain's automotive sector, then we should at least be driving a product they made. I asked for a 2 litre diesel Jaguar X-type, similar price, the lowest of the range, made by the good men and women of Liverpool.

The answer was 'no'. The Jaguar was 'not on the list'. Evidently it wasn't as 'green' as the hybrids. I reasoned to my auto minder that I thought it was important to support the companies that invest in our country by driving in a product made by the people of this country. Pressure should be put on the makers of those cars to make them more green, rather than simply shunning them – and I added that since I was about to do a lot of miles around the country, a 2-litre diesel on the motorway would be more efficient and a lot less polluting than a hybrid. Round London a hybrid is powered by electricity, but on the motorway, its fuel consumption and emissions are not competitive. I made it clear that, instead of the Jaguar, I would happily have a Honda (or Toyota or Nissan for that matter) made in the UK, thus rewarding the faith these world-class Japanese companies have shown in our country over the past three decades.

Still the answer was no and I was told that if I wished to press the case any more, it would have to be an issue for the Prime Minister.

So there we were, about to bother the leader of the fifth biggest economy on earth with the issue of what sort of twenty five grand car a junior minister could have. I knew, sadly, the bureaucrat was serious. So I tried to put some sanity into the frustrating exercise (somehow, I could not see my counterparts in Germany or France having quite the same problem!). I said that I would use my own Jaguar and charge the government 40p a mile – I could hardly say it without smiling. But still the answer was no. Apparently that arrangement would have been too elitist.

So I kept on fighting. The successors of those customers in the shop in Alvechurch in the sixties needed *someone* to fight for them.

Pat and I were invited to lunch with the Prime Minister and Sarah at Chequers. As we were leaving, and my Honda pulled up, he said, 'I thought you were getting a Jaguar'.

The leader of the second largest economy in Europe, staring down the barrel of a global economic meltdown had indeed been pestered about his Trade Minister's twenty five grand car. It was beyond belief.

***

So, I couldn't wait to get away from the lunacies of Westminster and Whitehall to begin my sales tour of the world, which would take me to 31 different countries on 45 different visits in 15 months. I knew I was promoting a relatively easy sell. UK PLC, for all its problems, has a stable currency, a steady administration and plenty of examples of successful inward investment – the perception is that we are good and fair-minded traders. We have plenty of friends in the world but I came to understand that there is one country that really doesn't like us … it's us! Our most effective enemy is ourselves; we tie our hands behind our backs and then enter the fight!

The 'non-dom' row proved the point.

The non-domicile rule has its origins in our history as an empire. It allows someone resident in the UK to cite another country as their real domicile and then although they pay tax on their UK earnings, they only pay UK tax on their earnings in the rest of the world if they 'remit' the money to the UK. It originally allowed those who owned land in Britain's dominions to escape tax on their colonial wealth unless they brought it back to Britain.

'Non-doms' as they're called always pay UK tax on their UK earnings. Of course, the high-profile of some fabulously wealthy football club owners or media figures fuelled the headlines about 'rich tax dodgers', a potent mix when added to the public concern about 'foreigners' and 'immigration', and an intoxicating delight when the pursuit of political popularity can so easily be assuaged.

In the autumn of 2007 the then Shadow Chancellor George Osborne announced that if they were elected, the Tories would introduce a tax on 'non-doms'. Great politics! Taxing rich diamond-toting foreigners with their flash cars and unpronounceable names played well in the Tory shires, the Tory press and that electoral nirvana, Middle England. And what did the government do? Instead of feeling strong enough to govern, to explain the real facts about the thousands in the banking sector, the university sector, the public sector, the catering and leisure sector who might be affected (and most certainly have an atmosphere created that told others they weren't welcome) they jumped at the chance to raise a few bob and pander to the perceived xenophobia of good ol' Middle England. A £30k annual levy regardless of income may have been good politics but it was lousy governing, damaging the country's ability to attract the very people we need here. Those who earned nothing overseas but still came here were of course not affected!

The very idea of 'non-doms' conjures a rich list of bankers, hedge fund managers and oil-rich Arabs who use our shores for some slight amusement and an immense tax break before they head off home to their respective mansions or palaces. But within that non-dom category, are thousands of overseas university lecturers, nurses, doctors and other assorted non-millionaires, who have simply decided to live and earn here at a particular stage of their professional lives.

It was one of our slightly richer non-doms who brought the issue into focus for me: a major Saudi investor in the UK employing thousands of people here, whose UK business paid UK tax which helped build UK schools and hospitals, sat next to me at a lunch in Ryadh on my ministerial visit to his country. He was complaining about the £30,000 non-dom levy and I observed that he could easily afford the money. He merely replied that of course he could afford £30,000, but that wasn't the point. He'd been made to feel unwelcome, and he felt this was the thin end of the wedge, the beginning of an anti-foreigner initiative in a country whose competitive advantage over the US or France was, in part, this very issue. He didn't need to say any more.

With one cheap gesture Britain had scored an expensive own goal.

Back in London, I was being interviewed by the *Financial Times* – and I talked about my upcoming visit to the US. I emphasised how important America was as a trading and investment partner, and finally the journalist asked how the current non-dom issue might overshadow the visit.

I said, 'if there were seven or eight reasons why you would invest in Britain more than other places, we've just lost one of them. If you put up one extra barrier to inward investment, or coming to work here, it makes my life more difficult.'

I had just said it how it was. A statement, in my view, of the obvious that most rational people would agree with. The following morning, I spent a couple of quiet hours with Pat before flying off to Los Angeles on a 12 day ministerial visit to the US, whence came a lot of wealth-creating non-doms.

When I eventually switched on my phone that morning, a fury of voicemails hit me. Evidently the Chancellor (through his increasingly agitated special advisors) had been trying to reach me from a conference in Japan on account of that morning's Leader in the *Financial Times*. My remarks made the front page headline as attacking the government's non-dom taxation policy. In number 11 thought-centre speak: 'Oh my God, the world has stopped turning!'

I delayed returning the voicemail storm for a few hours until I was en route to Heathrow. Alastair Darling, the Chancellor of the Exchequer, had by then calmed down. What wasn't impressive was 'the machine's' efforts in the form of the BERR Press Office issuing a statement purportedly from me without my consent or approval 'clarifying what I meant'! Thankfully, I managed to get the facts to the various editors personally in time to make sure I wasn't misquoted.

For every banker who earns a fortune, there are thousands of non-doms in this country who are working hard and paying UK tax, who have a little bit of income overseas, and suddenly they feel they are not as welcome.

I finally got through to the Chancellor in Tokyo – and he calmly told me that I was going against government policy and was worried the press would say I was being critical of him. My view was that businessmen and women reading the story – regardless of their political sympathies – would tell me that I was right. Inward investors would say that I was right. University vice-chancellors would say that I was right.

I finally told him that I was the man who had to get out there and sell this country and that we would have to disagree. He seemed to understand.

I knew I was right. For every banker who earns a fortune, there are thousands of non-doms in this country who are working hard and paying UK tax, who have a little bit of income overseas, and suddenly they feel they are not as welcome. So the wealth creators disappear. What a lack of policy focus on wealth creation that showed.

***

This frustrating inability to connect with business reality was constantly upheld by the Government's Obfuscation Department. Some months later, I was taking part in a *Question Time*-style evening in the North West, and I noticed a man from the UKTI Press Office in the audience. I asked him what he was doing there and he said he was here in case I 'had a problem'. I wondered what that might be. He said that I might say something that I shouldn't and, if that happened, he was there to help me say that I hadn't really said what I'd said. The taxpayer had paid this guy to travel hundreds of miles to deny something, which I would have already said to an audience and, more importantly, to the journalists who were there. What's more, it would be something I meant. I don't have a track record of not meaning what I say.

And sure enough, it happened. The question of the recent increase in capital gains tax came up. I spoke my mind and said that I could see how a small businessman or woman would think that the hike in tax from 10% to 18% was 'dreadful'.

That of course made more headlines next day, despite my minder's totally futile trip to be by my side, and the next day in London all hell broke loose, from the Treasury through BERR to the Leader of the House of Lords.

***

A couple of journalists rang me to ask if I thought I was failing as a minister. I said that in the party political, established view, I probably was. I was failing to turn up to vote and I was failing to walk down the road of convention. But, if they were to ask the business community and the embassies and the high commissions around the world in Britain's global markets they would get a very different and a very complimentary view.

I was addressing issues from a business perspective, and I considered that was my job as Trade Minister.

Thus far, I appreciate that this may all seem a bit naïve to the party machinists who strive to manage Whitehall, and to the party careerists who have experienced nothing else in their lives. I should have expected to experience obfuscation, obstruction, bureaucracy, condescension, and arrogance. Ah, yes, they would say, that's politics. Get used to it or get out. And that's OK is it? That's how it has to be, is it? Surely our great country could promote its trade around the world in a different way?

But I hadn't expected to witness the inefficiency and lack of urgency that needlessly put half a billion pounds of investment and 800 jobs on the line.

Bombardier is a great aerospace and engineering company based in Canada with large investments in the UK, where their Shortts subsidiary in Belfast is at the leading edge of technology using composites in aircraft manufacture. In 2008, they were looking for somewhere to make the wings of their new C110–130 series international business jet. The company was willing to invest £500 million in the project and the competition finally came down to Northern Ireland, or Wichita in the US, or Italy. For Ulster it was virtually the biggest investment they'd ever seen – with 800 jobs on the line. And not only was the future of the former Shortts factory in the balance, but the future of the UK's leadership in aerospace technology in terms of employment and skills.

Each country in the running for this investment had bid on the basis of providing loans to the manufacturer at commercial rates of interest, and had also set out its stall as to why it should be the preferred choice.

On the Saturday morning of that late Spring Bank Holiday of 2008, I got a call from Sir George Cox, who was on the Shortts board and he told me a rather depressing story. The parent company would be making their decision in the middle of the next week – five days away, and he was rather surprised that they'd heard nothing from BERR, particularly as Britain's bid was one of the last three. Sir George made it absolutely clear that he was not lobbying for more money or better terms for Bombardier, but merely to hear some sort of decision, yes or no, from Britain on its final offer.

Ringing the Prime Minister with every issue was not my style. That would have been my nuclear option but, while this was serious, this was not the time to press that button.

But one fairly fissile option was to light the fuse of a woman who epitomised the Ride of the Valkyries. Shriti Vadera had been a banker at UBS. Gordon brought her in as a special advisor, which is how I got to know her when I was at the CBI. When the Chancellor of the Exchequer became Prime Minister, Shriti became Baroness Vadera and a minister at the Department of International Development. Not a GOAT; she had too much previous for that and had been too much on the inside for that type of independence. Her staff called her 'The Shriek'. She was tough with the civil service staff and people skills were not what she was renowned for.

But, God bless her, she knew how to cut through Whitehall.

The United States is very generous with its aid programmes, but part of the deal is that American companies (after an internal competitive tender process) are used to do the work, and American jobs and profits increase accordingly. A win–win if ever there was one.

When I told her that Northern Ireland was possibly about to lose this contract for want of engagement, because Bombardier had so far received no final bid from the British government, what she did was way beyond Shriek. She corralled her civil servants into the office over that Bank Holiday weekend, and got the UK offer signed, sealed and delivered by the following Tuesday. An offer Bombardier bought. The contract kept 800 jobs alive, and re-affirmed Belfast's reputation as a world leader in aviation technology. The awful truth is that this skilled workforce could have been made redundant, if the normal system had had its way, had Sir George not called me on that Saturday morning and had I not made that call to the noble Baroness. But that is no way to run our inward investment delivery mechanisms.

***

Exporting our hard-earned money as Overseas Aid is something of which we should be proud, but the way it is done is wasteful. It neither fully satisfies our country's concerns for the world's needy, nor does it allow us to operate on a level playing field. The justification for sending our cash abroad is that if help is given to needy countries now, then it's cheaper than dealing with the more expensive consequences and symptoms of their poverty problems later on, from drug trafficking to terrorism, let alone the simple but painful issues of our fellow human beings in trouble and reaching out to our neighbour.

In 1997, one of the Blair government's first acts was to 'untie' the UK Overseas Aid programme, which meant that our donations became unconditional. But whilst this 'no strings attached' policy raised huge cheers from a left wing against perceived colonisation by cash, it meant that British companies weren't in line to get any of the work which the aid was funding– such as large construction projects or telecommunications infrastructure. No other major country in the developed world does this like we do.

The United States is very generous with its aid programmes, but part of the deal is that American companies (after an internal competitive tender process) are used to do the work, and American jobs and profits increase accordingly. A win–win if ever there was one. That doesn't happen in the UK. The recipient countries were and are still under no obligation to give any of the ensuing business back to the donors – the British taxpayer.

Worse than that, and quite apart from government corruption in many developing countries, there is no check on how the money is spent. Every time I challenged the Department for International Development I was told that the government did not interfere with the sovereign right of nations to handle the money as they wished. It was Labour Party policy and that was that. DFID thought of itself almost as an independent charity, only unlike charities the donations it received were not voluntarily given.

So a Labour government, elected to look after the interests of constituents, watched as a socialist shibboleth meant ministers and other MPs happily gave UK taxpayers' money away to fund projects from South America to Asia, from Africa to Eastern Europe. This, of course, helped someone there but also created jobs and wealth in France and America, in Japan and Germany and with no tangible return for the UK; what was worse, they couldn't see that there was anything wrong in doing it that way! DFID had become, as a party-management ploy, a charity, an aid agency; in short, it had gone rogue.

So the British taxpayer was for example giving £297 million a year to a nuclear armed India which is in the course of quadrupling its defence budget, has a space exploration programme and which will be one of the fastest growing economies in the world over the next few years.

If all this were to encourage bilateral trade then it might be a worthwhile investment but, so often, aid merely encourages a kind of national welfare dependency. I often wonder how a different approach to UK government aid – to Africa for instance – could deliver a better all-round result.

The Coalition government has promised a hard-headed review of overseas aid and it is good to see untied aid to the second biggest economy on earth, China, and to Russia being withdrawn. Other nations need our taxpayers' money a little more than they do! But the Overseas Aid budget had been spared the cuts which other government spending faces. Promises made in order to get elected is one thing, but I'm not sure that the hard-pressed taxpayer in Birmingham or Newcastle would be very impressed to know the government is not only spending our money with no quality control, but is not even creating business for Britain from it. To disguise that under the vague umbrella of some sort of moral international behaviour is disingenuous to say the least, and putting conditions on our hard-earned international aid is not on the Coalition's agenda, so UK business continues to miss out to its competitors in global markets.

***

As a minister with a business background, I was disappointed by the disregard that our elected representatives sometimes showed towards their shareholders – the voters. But I was surprised at how casually irrelevant the role of a Minister of the Crown is thought to be. I'd been picked up early one evening at Waterloo station for an event at the Hilton in Park Lane. It's usually a 20 minute drive. The driver gave me my ministerial red box and said that I needed to read and then sign the first document, which he would then take back to the office. No 10 needed it signed urgently.

I took it out of the case and it was sixty pages long. It would have been impossible to read it and even less understand it in the time the car would take to go from SE1 to the West End.

I rang my office and said that I was not going to sign it in the car but would take it home that night, carefully read it and, if all was fine, then sign it. They said that Number 10 needed it, and my department was under acute pressure to get it signed.

I refused to do it. My old senior partner at Edge & Ellison, a great man called John Wardle, preached constantly that no partner at his firm should ever sign *anything* that they didn't understand and were not prepared to support in front of a judge. My office informed Number 10 I wouldn't be signing it that night and they instructed us to send it back and they would get another minister to sign it quickly!

All Whitehall wanted was a minister's signature. Never mind who the minister was, or how much time the minister had given to the issue or its context or its importance.

In that short journey, from Waterloo to Park Lane, 20 minutes in a ministerial car – the Jaguar it had taken a Prime Minister to approve – I realised just what the system was about. You were expendable. You were needed to take responsibility, nothing more.

I found it one of the most depersonalising things in a job I had ever personally encountered.

One day the Prime Minister of the United Kingdom is telling me, as the new Trade Minister, that I'm entrusted to encourage the world to sign in to Britain, and then some unaccountable official says with equal apparent authority that I'm expected to be a cipher on some forgotten bit of regulation that I'm not even expected to read.

More than once I was told by some quite senior people that I was wasting my time to expect change.

All of which added to my underlying thought that the system does not accommodate business people to do the job. The culture was one of ducking accountability. If I found people were not 'cutting it' I was told they could be moved to another department but wouldn't be let go from the civil service. My particular problem would be sorted but the taxpayer would still be short-changed.

Something that my insight into Whitehall taught me was that if we are serious about value for money for the taxpayer we can do the job with fewer civil servants. That much is pretty obvious to a lot of people. But I would go one step further on the back of the experience I had, and that is to say that the fewer civil servants we do have need to be better and in turn trusted to be more responsible and essentially publicly accountable for their work. The Civil Service should also be able to say that if you've been helped, if you've been retrained and you're still not good enough, then you should go.

***

Aside from the general air of accepting second best, I'm not sure many business people would want to put up with the general day-to-day lunacies that come from the relentless churn of political stories and the need of the press to file copy.

I was giving a lunchtime speech in London to a Middle East audience of ambassadors and businessmen, and I set about my theme of Britain's eager embrace of globalisation, as an open nation of natural traders. And the UK welcomed anyone on their merit. I said ' We don't care about the colour of your skin, or which God you worship, we don't care about your name. Come here, create jobs, make money, pay tax. You are welcome.'

That afternoon, my press officer rang to say that a Sunday tabloid wanted to know if I had anything to say about the speech I had made where I'd said that I didn't care about Islam. I explained that of course I had said no such thing – and tried to explain that 'not caring about the God you worship' didn't mean that I didn't care about Islam – it meant that I felt people were free and welcome to worship whom they please where and when they want to. I thought that was pretty straightforward.

I had been in the East Midlands that morning at a UKTI event and had arrived at the lunchtime event just in time to deliver my after-lunch speech, something the organisers always knew and were quite happy with.

My press office told me that the same journalist had asked if I had anything to say about being late and if I'd had a drink before I'd spoken. I said not only had I not had a drink, but no lunch either! I know that it's difficult to believe that I miss lunch, but this was one of those times!

That Sunday, the story ran that Lord Digby Jones had insulted important Middle East investors because I'd said I didn't care about their religion and that my Press Office had been forced to deny that I had been drinking! And people read and presumably believe stuff like this!

I've always been happy to roll with the punches, but this was just wearing and time consuming. The government was creating its own whirlwind. Blair had excelled himself in spending on spin, and the army of Whitehall and contingent press officers hit a high of over 3000 during his time – all fuelling the furnaces of fact and fiction, and no doubt many other ministers found themselves spending far too much time feeding and counter-ing the media. That's the Westminster way, but I'm sure that if government asked serious businessmen or women however ex-perienced they may be with their companies, they would have a simple reply – why bother?

That cannot be good for Britain in the globalised, competitive economy of the twenty-first century – Asia's century, where

China and India walk to the beat of a different drum and create jobs and wealth on a scale that will effect every single person in our country through the next 100 years.

Nevertheless, the Trade Minister job is one of the most important in the country – promoting the creation of wealth which in turn generates tax and jobs which no other sector does. But there's a double bind about the role. No matter how exciting I tried to make UK PLC sound to overseas investors, I carried the ball and chain of Whitehall with me. If I threw down the 'Welcome to Britain' mat there would always be some ill-thought-out regulation or policy which would make life difficult for wealth-creating investment.

A media and, consequentially, party-political environment deals with the day to day and rarely looks at the bigger picture. Departures from the norm are viewed with suspicion because they are different and are interpreted as cracks in the façade of unity, not simply as things being done differently. It is destructively wearing. I think Britain is lucky to have the press it has in that, by and large, it keeps those in public life on their toes and basically honest; pricking the balloon of arrogance (something to which I am no stranger!) is a public service. But we somehow have to get some balance back.

***

Britain and UKTI can achieve so much when everyone rows the same boat in the same direction.

It was 2008, and Beijing was staging a fabulous Olympic Games. Sir Andrew Cahn, the CEO of UKTI, came to me with a great idea which the British Embassy in Beijing bought into at once.

We would take over the compound of the British Embassy for the duration of the Games and showcase what British business does really well. So we would have an event on aerospace engineering, one on IT technology, a day on automotive, a promotion on financial services, a day on the creative industries, an event on food manufacturing, a display of UK pharmaceuticals, a day for our training companies, a promotion for our amazing consulting engineers and architects, our universities and so on.

It was a marvellous concept. I agreed and signed off on it.

It was set up and ready to go. I said I would go out there for a couple of days at the end of the Olympiad plus the closing ceremony.

I was informed that I had to ask permission of the powers that be. I was then told by 'the Centre' that what with the Sports Minister going, plus the Olympics Minister and (for the closing ceremony and rightly) our Prime Minister, I could not go. There was no room in their plans and no space in the official allocation of tickets for the closing ceremony, and too many ministers in Beijing would attract accusations of junketing.

I told 'them' that I did not want to go to any of the events (even ones where Team GB were in with a chance of a medal) since my job (for which the taxpayer was paying) was to invite the world that was in Beijing to the UK Pavilion at our Embassy and sell them Brand Britain. I said that I believed very deeply in using the Olympiad to develop trade for our country and was so proud of what we can do that I would pay for my own hotel and flight and would accept quite transparently one of the many invitations I had received from various companies to be their guest at the closing ceremony. The rest of the time I would be 'doing my bit'. My Chinese visit would cost the taxpayer very little.

When my strength of feeling was understood and when I had dealt publicly with many newspaper enquiries as to whether I would be going and why, I was suddenly in the official party!

The whole thing went really well. Britain was in her Sunday best and everyone (not least those fabulous athletes who brought so much glory to our country and receive a fraction in a year of what an underachieving England footballer receives in a week) stepped up to the plate. I was amazed, and very pleased, by the number of overseas businesses, journalists and politicians interested in 'what the UK does these days'. Too many of them still thought we all run round in bowler hats in black taxis and on red buses working for banks and nothing else.

***

I was a transient GOAT in the job. But no one with political aspirations to reach the highest level wants to be Trade Minister for too long, because it involves being away from the Westminster beltway for extended periods. Which means not being around to vote, not being around to build a political career and not being around to plot in the tearooms.

That was entirely understandable, I hadn't needed to maintain a parallel Westminster existence with my overseas role, but just over a year of effectively living on an aeroplane nearly finished me off. I was exhausted and badly needed a couple of months off in the summer of 2008. I was overwhelmed by the kindness of so many ministers and other parliamentarians as I recovered my strength. Cathy Ashton, Judith Willcox and David Milliband were particularly kind and helpful.

Labour was tired, too. Brown had bottled the election in the autumn of 2007. He had always struck me as somebody who had definite innovative views about how he would run the country if he became Prime Minister, but it was all disintegrating as his authority ebbed away and the plotting began. It was an embodiment of a Shakespearean tragedy. A good number two, who has ached for the top job – he becomes number one then it all goes wrong. He'd pulled the levers to spend and borrow when he was Chancellor, which all worked when the country was running at top speed. But of course all that changed.

Politically he made a huge mistake. We forget now that, by September 2007, Cameron's standing was very low and Brown had had a couple of good months with his handling of the terrorist attacks, the foot and mouth outbreak and the floods. An election to give the new Prime Minister his own mandate was surely imminent.

Then he bottled it. It was a defining moment. People around him said he was indecisive. Labour broke into its old cabals. And a real opposition emerged, almost by default.

George Osborne, the Shadow Chancellor, stood up at the Tory Party Conference and said that he would, if given the chance, address Middle England's biggest grievance and cut inheritance tax. Whatever the rights or wrongs of that, it immediately put the Conservatives back in the political game. Neither Thatcher with Michael Foot and Neil Kinnock, nor Blair with William Hague and Iain Duncan Smith had real opposition. Brown, with his dithering, gave the reinvigorated Conservatives the ammunition they had so far lacked to attack him.

By mid-2008, when I saw senior figures like John Hutton and David Milliband with their heads in their hands about the leadership, I knew the already disjointed politics of Westminster was descending into a febrile and tribal atmosphere. It was no place for a non-party-political specialist trying to do things differently. I knew it was the right time to go.

Party politics was going to rule until the election, whenever that might be, and in many ways the experiment was over. 'Revert to type', the default option, was the order of the day. My successor took some months to be appointed, but then the former chairman of Standard Chartered Bank, Mervyn Davies, took up the challenge with great ability, and went into the Lords (but as a party member) albeit with a larger domestic financial services brief. Mind you, the ramifications of the collapse of Lehman Brothers was concentrating every mind. He might not have been quite as peripatetic as his predecessor but his success in the job (aided by one of the best permanent secretaries a minister could ever hope for in Sir Andrew Cahn) kept alive the chances that never again will the Trade and Investment job go to a career politician. Getting someone from the business community to take up the challenge for the good of the country with little or no pay, operating in the goldfish bowl of political life and assailed by a system that resists change and a media that suspects it, is an entirely different matter. I wish Lord Stephen Green, former chairman of HSBC all the luck in the world as the next 'trustee of the mantle'. An excellent choice, another person from global business, skilled and experienced in how business works. He is the next man on the rope, from a gene pool of non-party-political talent originally conceived by Gordon Brown. I hope the former Prime Minister's foresight in this matter will reap great rewards for the country for years to come.

***

I found a deep respect for Britain in the countries with which we need to partner, and from whom we need inward investment. While we are generally liked in the world, our real opposition is alive and well and living in the UK. The one country that really doesn't like us … is us! And the pull of domestic politics means that senior ministers might make the odd foray into commercial diplomacy, but Whitehall still regards business with disdain.

I found a deep respect for Britain in the countries with which we need to partner, and from whom we need inward investment.

Our own government, whether elected politicians or their enforcers, the civil service, must not suffocate our lifeline into the twenty-first century – the businesses of Britain and their natural ability to create wealth, taxation and jobs.

I thoroughly enjoyed my time representing my country in its overseas markets. It had been a privilege to promote Brand Britain all the time everywhere. It is hard work and not without its frustrations but the feeling of making a difference for UK business was very real. And, after all, that is what I was there to do.

CHAPTER 4

EDUCATION, EDUCATION, EDUCATION?

I'm at an assembly of teachers and local businesses in the main hall of a West London secondary school. It's 2003. I was there as a guest speaker on one of the CBI initiatives which was trying to build a practical link between business and the classroom. I began to speak about the vital importance of pupils becoming an employable generation to take our country into the twenty-first century.

One of the teachers, all hair, jeans and corduroy jacket, interrupted. He said if I thought he was going to spend his career producing cannon fodder for capitalism then I must have been joking.

I thought of that teacher a couple of years later as I visited facilities in Ho Chi Minh City and Hanoi in Vietnam, where 3000 young engineers write the software of the 3G mobile network base stations for Alcatel. I was in a country which knew all about real cannon fodder and the genocide beyond that, and yet here were 21-year-olds writing their complicated, high-tech trade in an immaculate workplace. No sweatshop, just the quiet enthusiasm of expert youth at work, earning, in relative terms, good money.

If the nineteenth century belonged to Britain and the twentieth to the US, with due respect to the immense economic powerhouse that is today's Brazil, the twenty-first belongs to Asia. And at the top of the pile of social concerns in Asia, which I've seen on many visits, is education.

Not every Asian family does this, but there's a general thrust for the improvement of the next generation. They've seen that educated people have a wealthier lifestyle and that those with the qualifications tend to be healthier, live longer and improve their family's circumstances. What a simple and profitable philosophy that is.

The parents of those children in that HD software factory were still working at least eight hours a day on the land, but they had decided to invest for the future, and that future was their children's education. They are a living exemplar of a war-ravaged economy which is now a successful emerging market, and one that is never again going to go backwards.

If the nineteenth century belonged to Britain and the twentieth to the US, the twenty-first belongs to Asia. And at the top of the pile of social concerns in Asia, which I've seen in many visits, is education.

Let me tell you a quick story. I was sitting in the back of a limousine being driven between appointments in Bahrain. The driver was looking at me in his rear-view mirror. I asked him where he came from. He said he was from Chennai in India and, if the job worked out over two years, his wife and family could join him. In the meantime he sent money home every month. He was proud to tell me the money was educating his son. 'What does he want to do when he leaves school?' I asked. 'One day he will be sitting where you are, not where I am', he replied. I wish everyone in Britain had heard that statement of sacrifice, dedication and ambition.

These stories from Vietnam and Bahrain provide a sad contrast with Britain, the state of education, and the value that is placed on it, in this country.

***

As I mentioned in the first chapter, in the late nineties, one of our leading statisticians, Sir Claus Moser had been tasked with preparing a report on the levels of the UK's basic education and skills.

What he'd found was staggering.

According to Moser, one in five adults was functionally illiterate. Moser's next example was a poster for a pop concert, taking place at the Birmingham National Exhibition Centre.

One in sixteen adults – that is 16% of the population available for work, could not work out from the poster where the concert was to be held.

When it came to numeracy, 25% of adults couldn't work out how much change they would expect from £2 if they'd bought £1.58p of groceries.

I could not believe my eyes.

Then there is the official statistic, which adds to this list of educational failure – nearly half of all the young people who take GCSEs don't get a grade C or above in English and Maths. Which means they are not fit to work in the majority of jobs in the real world, beyond the classroom.

Moser's report was published in 1999. Government ministers have often claimed that much has changed since then. That's not what the country's employers are telling me, even now. And while that sad GCSE statistic varies a few per cent either way each year, it remains virtually the same. Indeed in summer 2010 the government announced that 20% of children aged ten were still functionally illiterate; sadly about to become the next statistical proof that Moser's findings haven't changed in a decade. Indeed, it is wrong in so many ways for this Coalition government to axe the Every Child a Reader programme and the Train to Gain scheme. The saving of public money begins with ridding the nation of the blight of illiteracy, not abolishing the very programmes that help to do so!

Ministers, and some educationalists, have often said that the failure to get above grade C in Maths and English is not an indication of functional illiteracy.

But if a young person turns up for a job or an apprenticeship, expecting to be taught how to operate a lathe or to weld, and is unable to read the instructions, then that spells functional illiteracy to me.

Moreover, if GCSEs don't serve to prove a level of functional literacy, then what are they testing? What is the purpose of these exams? Employers need benchmarks, standards universally accepted and understood, against which to measure suitability for further training or employment. Colleges of Education, which are so vital in taking 16-year-olds out of school and skilling

There have always been people who can't read, write or count... but the developed world doesn't have the jobs for those people any more

them vocationally for trades that will provide a lifetime's opportunity for work, have to spend the first term teaching too many of their students to read, write and count. What a waste of time, money and effort, and a negative impact on the productivity of the country.

The knock-on effects of this to the UK are wide and far reaching in the economy, in society, in crime and even in our health system.

There have always been people who can't read, write or count. In fact, 70 years ago, the statistics were probably worse. But in the past these people would have found work in the fields in Somerset, or worked in a pool of oil under the sump of an Austin on a production line in Longbridge. They went into the shipyards of Glasgow and the steelworks of South Wales. The pits of South Yorkshire and the mill towns of Lancashire provided work for thousands of them. These people were always there but they always had something worthwhile to do which gave them money to take home at the end of the week. So they felt needed, they were part of a community, they preserved their dignity and self-respect and they earned money. This is not just a British issue – we could equally be talking about Germany, France or the US.

But the developed world doesn't have those jobs for those people any more. The world of work has changed forever. According to Microsoft, three quarters of jobs in the private sector demand IT skills. You could argue that there are still such jobs in the public sector. But as we attempt to pay down our enormous debts, the government and the taxpayer are going to demand more for less among the millions who work in the public sector. It is necessary that they become more productive and efficient; that will mean fewer people doing more, and doing it differently. They will have to feel confident enough to be trained to do something else, to espouse IT skills if they don't have them already. They must embrace change and that is virtually impossible for scared and unskilled people. They will need to understand and to learn new ways. Many will need to make the transition from public to private sector. They won't be able to do any of that if they can't read, write or count.

The change in the world of work in the last generation has meant an increasing section of society without any realistic prospects of a job, and each year another batch of unskilled youngsters is pushed out from the classroom, with no real chance of finding decent work. This so often leads to feelings of inadequacy and low self-esteem and, in frustration, people will often turn to drink, drugs or even crime. They become obese from a lack of self-esteem, don't care for themselves, or those around them. It is this pattern that means in one way or another, poor education can result in higher costs to our NHS. They are also a drain on our benefits system, and will eventually need to be housed, at a further cost to the taxpayer.

So in all important perspectives in Britain – economic, social, health, crime, public sector reform and private sector success and survival – basic education has failed the country. I cannot believe that some teachers find it acceptable that their charges – those young people upon whom the future of our country depends – can leave school without being able to read or count.

***

In looking for solutions to this downward spiral we need to explore and understand the path that has brought us here, over the past forty years.

One of the educational routes out of a challenged socio-economic background was the grammar school. Here was an opportunity for most children who passed their 11-plus and then stayed the course until they were 18. There would be the chance to go to university, or enter employment at a much higher level than might have been expected. They could move onto higher ground for ever.

Those who didn't make that early grade went to secondary modern schools, which many in Britain's class structure thought were educational dustbins. They were not, although far too many of them were simply not good enough and not attuned to the changing needs of post-war Britain. The socialist argument in the sixties was not that we needed to make the secondary moderns better, or that we should have apprenticeships starting at 14. There was no thought to improve the practical and academic achievement for those who at the age of 11 had failed a method of selection based on intelligence and mental ability.

Instead, government decided to abolish what they regarded as an elitist system and went for the lowest common denominator: the comprehensive system. At a stroke, we'd stopped believing in winners.

We stopped believing that it's important to be first. Children got the message that everyone's the same. Striving to be the best didn't matter and went unrewarded. Everyone could have prizes in a dumbed-down, enforced, egalitarian educational experiment. Only this experiment was for real and, for one generation at least, the ability to compete in a changed world was impaired forever. Our competitors in the increasingly globalised economy were not adopting the sort of education that strives to level rather than to achieve.

At same time, the sixties' education revolution fostered a politicised class of teachers, many of whom had had an easy entry into the profession through teacher training colleges, which had much lower entry standards than the universities.

Britain should be in the game of maximising individual talent, not subordinating it to a common standard that excuses poor performance by both pupil and the system.

So many of our schools have ended up with sports days where there are no winners, where everyone who turns up on the start line gets an equal prize. Why did grading get such a thumbs down? It was decreed that no one would know, or should know, whether they were first, second or third.

Having winners obviously means there will also be losers. These 'losers' should not be left alone under any system. They *must* at all costs be taught to read, write, count and operate a computer, no matter how long it takes. Then they should be helped to maximise their talent in a subject where they can win. Nurtured in something that they are good at and can excel in. Communities, employers, teachers and parents must work together to find that thing that a child can do well, and then take him or her to being first in it, and celebrate the success.

Britain should be in the game of maximising individual talent, not subordinating it to a common standard that excuses poor performance by both pupil and the system.

State education too often decrees that there will be no winners so that we can't have losers. Of course there are grades in exam papers, but they have been successively dumbed down, especially at 'A' level. Many years after my own attempt at A levels I dug out my old papers and compared them with the sort of exams today's students sit. Mine were now the equivalent of an examination after the first year at university.

Today's A-level students work harder and are under more pressure than their counterparts of forty years ago. But the basics are not generally there in the same way and the whole system has regressed.

Teachers must be, and be seen to be, professionals. Professionals operate to a code where the client comes first. They don't go on strike. Being seen to put their own interests ahead of those of their pupils is route one to losing society's respect. If teachers had greater respect in society, then more parents might involve themselves to do their vital part in their children's education. Home support is essential if we are to have better educated children, fit for a competitive, globalised economy.

Official figures from the General Teaching Council in 2010, showed that only eighteen teachers had been dismissed for incompetence in the past 40 years. But a BBC *Panorama* investigation at the same time reported that there were as many as 17,000 struggling teachers – a claim backed by the former chief inspector of schools Chris Woodhead who, even in 1995, estimated there were 15,000 failing teachers,

In any profession, it's important to put the client or the customer first. So who is the teaching profession's client? It is the pupil who is the teacher's professional responsibility, and whose interests must come first. But there is another interested party – the customer of the education system – the future employer, be it in the private or public sector. The world out there wants a young person who's been through an educational system that delivers them fit for the world of work in the twenty-first century.

Since 2000 when I started at the CBI I have seen such a marked improvement in the standard of teaching and the old cliché 'show me a good head teacher and I'll show you a good school' rings true more than ever. The vast majority of teachers now 'get it'. They deserve the support of all of us. But the battle for the regaining of society's respect for teaching, and teaching's reclaiming of the professional ground, is still to be won. No classroom should have a politicised agenda that suits a teacher's personal agenda.

The teacher's role is to explain both sides of any argument and equip the pupils with the reasoning power to make their own decisions, and more than anything else equip them for the world of work in Asia's century.

***

Outside the classroom, there's also been an abrogation of an essential part of children's all round education, and that begins in the home – parental responsibility.

I have visited many schools where the school lunch was the only hot meal of the day for most of the children. I have seen young children who could recite many TV commercials, but couldn't read, because parents have dumped them in front of the television for several hours a day, virtually from birth.

Many parents just don't bother to help with their children's education and these children are being let down first and foremost by their parents.

I'm not a parent myself, and so I can't speak from personal experience. But in my visits to schools it was apparent to me that the idea of opening any sort of book at home or outside school was a completely foreign act to many of these children. This lack of encouragement at home must be partly to blame for a lack of reading ability. Many parents just don't bother to help with their children's education and these children are being let down first and foremost by their parents. Too many feel that 'they' – the state, 'the social' – will provide, including teaching their own blood to read, write and count.

We are where we are partly because the culture in this country is increasingly one where parents are shunning responsibility for their offspring's education. At the same time, politicians have destroyed the country's ability to select on merit and nurture talent for the good of society in a changed world.

But now there's a much more insidious form of selection. After all the levelling down and non-winning culture of comprehensive education, the choice of a state school for your children is increasingly based on money.

A good state school forces up the house prices in its area, because everyone else wants their children to go there, too. Some parents migrate to qualify, whereas others are forced to lie about where they live. Those who can afford a house, move. The majority stay where they are, and have to take pot luck with the quality of the school which is in their catchment area. By seeking to destroy the process of 'selection by ability', the socialists have created a far more destructive method of selection for a child's education – not ability, but money.

Ironically, one of the principal architect of the sixties' destruction of the grammar school system, and the leg-up it provided for so many, was educated at one of our finest public schools, St Paul's. Shirley Williams aimed to create an inclusive, cohesive society by getting rid of grammar schools in favour of comprehensives. Her partner in this destruction, the Labour Minister Anthony Crosland, who was educated at Highgate School and at Trinity College, Oxford, according to his wife Susan said 'if it's the last thing I do, I'm going to destroy every f***ing grammar school in England. And Wales. And Northern Ireland.'

It turned out to be one of the worst ever failures of public policy in the history of our country. The system which was designed for the lowest common denominator fulfilled its potential and, in doing so, blighted the life chances of millions of youngsters. As a result, it has done untold damage to the global competitiveness of the UK as it arms itself for the enhanced productivity battle that is Asia's century.

So, after 11 years of free, compulsory, full time education half the country's school leavers can't functionally read, write or count.

We have all paid taxes to fund those eleven years, and the system has failed. And it has failed the teacher as much as the child. No teacher wants young people to leave school ill-equipped for the world of work. We need to work out a way of future employers, in both the private and public sectors, taking greater ownership of education.

One answer from the Coalition is for government to put up the money for local groups to plan and run their own school. That might work where there are pushy parents and people who've bought into the idea. 'Owning' one's own school sounds quite attractive but it would also involve hard work from parents, and a lot of it would be voluntary. Local small businesses should take this opportunity to get more involved with the school down the road.

The idea is fine for the well-off and the committed, but how is this going to work in the country's challenged areas, where the worst of the problems are?

Academies were an excellent initiative of Blair's government, although they were poorly supported by his successor. This initiative has thankfully been expanded enormously by the Coalition government, and is very popular. The academies are funded jointly by public funds and private philanthropy, but crucially they are managed on a basis free from party politics. Local authorities can't interfere; it's not their business. Parents and kids flock to them.

Today, more and more academies are opening, many with a specialist theme – from engineering to creative industries – providing a clear route for giving challenged but bright kids a break. We did of course have such a culture in education two generations ago – grammar schools.

The real test is to get parents who have shown no interest in their children's education, who want no acceptance of responsibility, to understand the significance and importance of education. It's everyone's education system. Our children's success will lead to a society which is greatly enriched in many different ways.

In order to achieve this we need to elevate education in the nation's agenda. We need a massive national campaign. We must get people to understand that the training and education of their children is as important as the World Cup, or as what happened on their favourite soap last Wednesday, or as important as their rights to welfare benefits. That is where this journey must start.

***

The media must help. Imagine *Coronation Street* or *Emmerdale* with strong story lines crafted by their writing talent about setting up and running a small business with success and ambition, moulded into the style and plot lines which a huge audience loves. And the key to it would plainly be skilling up and training young people, not the sexual or bullying proclivities of the owner of the business.

The writers may well have to change their prejudices. The serial killer on *Coronation Street* was a businessman, the murderer on *EastEnders* was a businessman and the one big crook on *The Archers* was a businessman. Not the most favourable light in which to reflect business success or the need for self-improvement through skilling in business.

Business people aren't all good, nor are they all bad. Business is about success and failure, which creates exactly the sort of long running stories which would suit a soap format. And business is often box office. Apart from *The Apprentice* and *Dragon's Den*, think of the old blockbusters like *Dynasty* and *Dallas*. If gardeners and farmers listen to the occasional agricultural hint on the *The Archers*, a business slant to a storyline now and again might just bridge the gap between the Rover's Return and the reality of earning that pint. We must pay our way in the world, be globally competitive. It all comes back to education.

For some reason, unfathomable in this changed world, the school leaving age is still set at 16. Many of these kids are now physically so much more mature and are often disruptive in class, they disrupt the pupils that want to get on, and they feel that the classroom is no longer for them. One reason is that teaching basic literacy and numeracy all seems to stop at 11 or 12 years old which means some pupils go through the next four years ill-equipped to learn. The practical effect of that is that the children have no interest in other subjects because they simply can't read the material. That's where destructive boredom begins.

We need a form of coercion that prevents children leaving school if they can't read, write or count; and, increasingly, have an acceptable level of IT literacy as well. The National Curriculum league tables must change to accommodate this.

Those who want to leave school and don't have the necessary basic skills, should carry on learning until they can. This must be the responsibility of the education authorities and parents and the launch of such a project would need to be underlined by a national advertising campaign and a degree of sanction.

It may sound far-fetched now, but cultures can change. Think about the Drink Drive campaign. People used to boast about how much they could drink and still drive. Nowadays people would be ashamed to say that. So why can't we make reading, writing, and operating a computer something that *everyone* promotes in a culture geared towards success?

For those studying for their GCSEs, I would propose another optional strand to their education. There would be an employer down the road who would take pre-sixteen teenagers into a job for two or three days a week. That scheme would combine with a local college which would give them the theoretical part of the training, and the result would be a ticket. That ticket might be in secretarial administration, welding or plumbing, farming or electrical engineering, but it would allow a young person to start earning a bit of money. The employer would be helped by the taxpayer to do this; it benefits us all that a young person is employable. This practical enhancement of further education would be a vital link between 14 or 16-year olds and the real life of work. And the risk-averse gods of 'Health and Safety' and the insurance companies would have to change approach to allow this to happen.

***

In times of stress, people look to the totems in their society. Their God, their football team – and they also look to their employer, so often the source of payment, a social life and of feeling needed. So the role of the employer, public or private, should be the hub from which go the spokes out into the community. Training should thus be compulsory, for both the teenagers and employers, with government meeting the cost – a good investment in the future for the taxpayer if ever there was one.

Understanding other cultures is essential to winning the global competitiveness battle, and understanding a country's language is the entry to understanding its culture. And the ticket should include a grounding in science and a foreign language. Understanding other cultures is essential to winning the global competitiveness battle, and understanding a country's language is the entry to understanding its culture. The barriers of ignorance and its child, prejudice, could be knocked down more easily if other cultures were better understood. Moreover, you always stand a better chance of selling something to someone if you afford them the respect of at least trying to talk to them in their language. But we must move our language horizons on from the familiar, but increasingly internationally unused, French and German to the languages of the twenty-first century – Spanish and Chinese – alongside the global language of business, air travel and IT – English. These three are the languages of the next hundred years and lessons in them should be available in every community.

Small businesses, the huge wealth-creating backbone of UK PLC, would campaign against compulsory training because it would be another cost for them. I understand that. They would see it as another deluge of regulation and red tape. Another intrusion of Big Government. And unions would love it; an excuse for more power for them in the workplace disguised as training representatives.

But the private sector (especially the small business end) has had its chance over many years.

If they think that training is expensive, they should just try ignorance!

If they think that training is expensive, they should just try ignorance!

We should bribe small business, through tax breaks and financial help and then make it compulsory. The employer is then the hub of a wheel-and-spoke operation, which encircles home and education, and should provide a worthwhile and, let's hope, a prosperous partnership.

***

We are very fortunate at the other end of the spectrum from basic training. University education is superb in this country. We have a cluster in the top ten best universities in the world and many others have very good reputations worldwide. No other country on earth (after the US) has as many universities in the World Top 100 as in the UK.

But this excellence is under threat from cuts in funding and so many young people who have excellent grades cannot get a place to go on to higher education. So, why not bring the time taken to undergo a conventional degree course down from three years to two? Just because universities 'have always done it this way' doesn't mean it must always be that way. If holidays were to be shortened and lecture programming reworked such a move would be easily achievable. So, much more productive activity can be put across the sector's fixed cost.

We also need to give added value to vocational qualifications. It might not seem as if an apprenticeship in plumbing has the same status as a master's degree in nuclear engineering and, in academic terms of course, it doesn't. But both the plumber and the nuclear scientist are serving society with their expertise – and of course earn money and pay tax.

When Charles Clarke was Education Secretary he said that getting 50% of school leavers to university would be a benchmark of success. What a regrettable thing to say, because it implies that the 50% who don't go to university are failures, in the eyes of a society that must *not* be thinking that way.

That makes anything but a degree appear second best. I have no idea what percentage of the population should go to university – but I do want to live in a society where everybody can, if they work hard enough and are good enough. There are many who will never be suited to a university education, and we must add value to alternative vocational qualifications. Many a training journey can start with something that is more vocational but has as its eventual qualification a degree.

But a vocational qualification should be regarded as an achievement and a standard in its own right. In so many cases we're paying for children to go to university for a moderate degree in a subject of little relevance, who come out of it at 21 as no more fit for purpose for the world of work than they were when they were 18.

Higher education is not free. Why should a taxpayer, who will derive little or no benefit from a student's three-year attendance at university (and that will put more money in the student's pocket over a lifetime of working) pay for all of it? The student's loan to pay for tuition fees does not have to be repaid unless or until good money is being earned and surely this contribution is fair to all concerned.

This next generation is going to need even more skill flexibility. My father had two jobs in his life. I've had three or four main ones – the next generation may have six or seven, some of which will require retraining. There will be no shame in redundancy as work patterns, global needs and capacity change, as public sectors' requirements alter. There will be shame in not being skilled-up ready for the next job. Learning will become a life long occupation – not simply something for five to sixteen or twenty-one-year olds. People will go back to university when they're over 40, a sales manager who's been let go at 52 might go back to a college to study carpentry. Colleges of further education and universities will need to build this into their syllabi and the staff may well be teaching large numbers of students who are many years their senior.

And students, young or old, need to understand that this is enhancing their suitability for work. The workforce is going to be clocking in until they are well over 70 – and we all need plumbers. Someone born today will probably live into their 90s; you wouldn't bet against it, and the professional odds-layers, the actuaries, certainly don't.

***

In Britain we cannot have a 90-year life expectancy supported by just 40 (or fewer) years of work; and the workforce must be flexible in its work patterns and in its learning attitudes.

We all need life skills, too. 'Get your hands out of your pockets. Look me in the eye. The pleasure of earning a living is not for everyone but you. Turn up to work on time. Turn up to work at all.' That's the sergeant major stuff. But you'd be surprised how much of that, according to employers I speak to, is necessary. What the potential work force needs to understand is that if they don't show themselves as fit for the world of work, and wanting it, then no employer in whichever market place, public or private, is going to give them a job. The National Curriculum must contain courses on the essential aspects of being fit for purpose.

Now this may sound beyond simplistic, but it will need to be spoon-fed to a generation who have become accustomed to a world where competitiveness and improvement are for other people. That is changing – not because of a new Coalition government in power, but because there is a growing realisation that it has to. The nation is frankly on the edge of bankruptcy. No country can allow the indolent, especially the able indolent, to wallow in state benefit land. Economics will dictate that those who don't wish to work, will get nothing. And unlike in the past, getting nothing from a job will not mean getting something from benefit. The efforts of Iain Duncan Smith to forge a new realisation of this twenty-first century fact of life are to be applauded.

Teachers will need to buy into this completely.

We will need a different type of teacher in certain schools. According to *The Times*, there were 251 assaults on teachers by pupils in 2010. Of these, 45 had to go to hospital. Almost half of all teachers leave the profession within five years of qualifying. The biggest reasons cited are abuse, violence or threat of violence from aggressive pupils. So we need teachers who can stand up to a class of sixteen-year-old thugs who may well want to get their knives out. Perhaps we should have two teachers in the classroom or different types and with different skill sets. You

According to *The Times*, there were 251 assaults on teachers by pupils in 2010. Of these, 45 had to go to hospital. Almost half of all teachers leave the profession within five years of qualifying. The biggest reasons cited are abuse, violence or threat of violence from aggressive pupils.

could understand neither of those teachers wanting to be there. They may well need a guard on duty as well. The enforcement of tougher discipline is long overdue. Perhaps the sixteen-year-olds should not have been in that classroom in the first place.

There are not enough male teachers in primary education. They are not as rare as hen's teeth but the simile is not far off the mark. We must introduce programmes to get more men into primary teaching, including different and better pay levels, no matter how politically incorrect it may be. Boys need role models, they need what in some situations is the only adult male they encounter in a stable situation. They will move into secondary education with more confidence and self-esteem if a man has had at least some influence on their education. A young lad from a home with a single mum and transient male visitors, who only has a schoolteacher/pupil relationship with a female, will often be prey to damaging influences as he grows up, and poor concentration spans and loss of confidence can result.

The system, the educationalists, should be sorting this out. This has to be part of the national campaign, because we have no choice if Britain is going to survive, never mind become successful again. It will need greater investment from the taxpayer but the alternative will cost us all so much more.

***

We also need to get heavy with parents. Coercion to care for their children in their home is difficult, and of course shouldn't be necessary, but maybe we need to engage where the parents spend their time. Their local workplace, their pub, the bingo hall. The local footballers who earn the locals' annual salary in a week, should play a part, as a part of their contract. We must have constant community and role model involvement in the education process. We need a GCSE in parenting, and perhaps some benefit bribes for those who keep their children on the page of learning and training (and possibly the threat of benefit withdrawal for those who do not). It's easy to assess – can they read, write, count and operate a computer by the time they leave school?

Once again there's going to be a big problem in the challenged areas, not just with the parents who don't care, but with the different ethnic groups that feel that they have even less of a share in our country's future, or a wish to take part in this.

One of the greatest mistakes of the last 50 years is that we've been trying to build multicultural Britain, where we should have built ethnically-integrated Britain.

Integration means that the colour of your skin or the god you worship deserve proper respect, but you will speak English. Your children will be educated at the same sort of school as everyone else. You will be treated the same as everyone else, not differently, in a land where a unified country comes first and individual race or religion is of secondary importance from a government (at any level, local or national) point of view.

The ethnic communities are rightly very keen to teach their own sacred texts. We need to use that admirable ethic of training, concentrating and learning and adapt it to the benefit of the more general community, to work towards improved secular educational advancement as well.

There will, of course, always be a section of society that will never be interested, or reached, by this. Any form of legal coercion would merely fill the prisons with people who shouldn't be there. That's a failure.

What we need to do, though, is to eat away at the edges of that hard core and attack the problem locally, not with social workers but with business people, public sector employers, ethnic community leaders, media people, sportsmen and women – people to whom they can relate.

We will never completely succeed, but that should never be an excuse for not trying. If, year by year, a few families can be 'saved' through the education system in its broadest sense, from the spiral of benefits and parental breakdown – perhaps the idea will catch on with other families in the community. And once it's the norm not to be unemployed, the best evangelists are the recently converted. They become part of the solution. Then we have a chance of making the step change.

I understand why youngsters join a gang – a gang gives them an order, a strata, they know where they stand, they get respect and give respect, they have orders, they know what is expected of them, they are praised when they deliver and they're punished when they don't. A gang gives them a structure they can relate to and they have order in their lives.

There is another organisation which provides a structure and it's called the army. You can see what many young people are aching for is a more ordered, structured way of life.

There is another organisation which provides a structure; it's called the army. You can see what many young people are aching for is a more ordered, structured way of life. The past 50 years has taken away those structures in our society. Sometimes it's been beyond control, because of the collapse of the big manufacturing employers, and sometimes because of policy such as comprehensive education.

I am not proposing National Military Service, but a compulsory, paid, one-year course to be served by everyone in the country between 16 and 19. Not military service and no one will be made to pick up a gun. It would be much more than a boot camp and it would be designed to maximise each individual's potential, to build on relationships of trust with their colleagues, to find what each of them is good at, to test and push, so that self-respect and self-esteem increase. This would not be set up or run by 'school' or 'social workers', but again by people who are trained, perhaps in business, but also in motivational techniques and physical fitness, and who would also maintain very tight discipline throughout.

There would be legal coercion to do the course, and those who didn't would be committing a criminal offence, just like the draft.

There would be no excuse for not doing this because of someone's means or qualifications, background or orientation, ethnic group or religion. There would be no conscientious objecting to it, because this is about being a participant in the United Kingdom, understanding one's rights but also one's responsibilities. It would be a ticket into UK adult society which everyone from the richest kid to the poorest, Muslim and Jew, talented or challenged, must have, with very few exceptions.

It will be a very difficult learning curve for teachers and parents. But just a small shift in the national attitude would at least put something of a better life within the grasp of more people, who will have been given some decent tools for the gritty reality of making a living.

Not everyone is going to be a Richard Branson or a Philip Green. When I was at the CBI one of the bits of spin from the Blair government was that they constantly associated business with personality entrepreneurs. I can understand why they did it because

Branson, Green or Stelios Haji-Ioannou are box office. They're prepared to open their mouths, they're attractive, inspirational, and they are of course successfully and openly wealthy.

I could see why Blair wanted to associate himself with that sort of person, but the problem is they are the exception rather than the rule.

Teachers, the media, children at school and at university have to understand that so many worthwhile jobs in the private sector have nothing to do with being an entrepreneur. So much of business is sheer hard work. It's preparation. It's putting in the grunt. It's doing your exams. It's turning up to work on time. My worry is that kids who express an interest in business, who say they want to make a lot of money and be like Richard Branson, don't of course say they want to be a quality engineer at Rolls Royce or a departmental head at Vodafone. But for British business to survive, to create the profits and the jobs and generate taxes for our country, those are exactly the sort of jobs which are vital. The entrepreneurs can think the big thoughts for the future and take the big risks, but there's always an important business behind them which needs skilful running.

That's why we need to dovetail business into the classroom. You might be studying to be an engineer, and GKN might want you as an engineer, but what they also want from you is a knowledge of what a money-making concern actually is. The CBI ran a very good initiative along those lines in the West Midlands, called 'Business in the Classroom'. A firm would go into a school asking the pupils if they would like to do a real live piece of work for the business, under the company's supervision. It wasn't just an exercise, it was for real and, most importantly, the children developed an understanding of how what they were doing would fit into the overall running of a company. They knew it was relevant and important. They also had a first hand view of how a company works, how people are managed, what cash flow means in reality, what the environmental concerns are and all the other components that comprise a business. They did something that was appreciated much more than just making the tea.

Similar schemes, nationwide, would be invaluable for fixing Britain for the future.

***

Teachers also need to revisit our past. History is not a compulsory subject after 14 (unlike in the US or Japan or most of the EU) and in 2009 some 220,000 candidates sat GCSE history, only 4% of all GCSEs taken. More people sat psychology at A level than history. We must ensure the next generation can put our nation's history into context and learn from it. The accumulated experience of yesterday can do so much to help the decision makers of tomorrow. But too many, when they are taught in school, are taught a fashionable disapproval of our often violent history, with no proper historical context.

In the National Curriculum, history should be taught in a non politically-correct way. A good example would be Britain's involvement with India. We did many things there of which we should be ashamed, but it must be seen within the context of the times. India now is a manufacturing and high-tech superpower with an economic prowess which is worth billions of pounds a year to the UK. Thousands of jobs for the UK economy now depend on India.

When I was on a ministerial trip to India, I held a news conference coincidentally near to the site of an infamous massacre of Indian people by the British. My officials warned me that it was still a very sensitive topic there, and I would be expected to apologise for what had happened over 150 years ago. The official British line was that there would be no apology.

The first question, sure enough, was, would I apologise for the massacre? I said that I would be prepared to do that – at which all the journalists poised their pens, and collectively my officials put their heads in their hands – but, I said, on one condition. My great-great-great-grandfather was called Anthony Boston. He was on duty in Lucknow the night the Indian mutiny started. An Indian came up behind him and cut his throat. I said to the assembly, 'you apologise for murdering my great-great-great-grandfather, and I'll apologise for what we did.'

Down went all the pens, my officials let out a great sigh of relief and I said, 'now shall we talk about what we really ought to be talking about?'

Which was, how were our two great nations going to trade with each other, invest in each other's economies, enjoy and make the most of each other's immigration so that we could both build better countries and, through commercial intercourse, help our people compete in a globalised, competitive world. We need to learn the lessons from our past – remembering it and honouring it whilst looking forward and upwards. It is the only way.

We must stop apologising for the past. We certainly did some pretty horrible things, but teachers need to explain what were the standards of the day, and what other countries did and, indeed, what some groups of natural inhabitants in those countries we colonised did to some of their own. Dogmatic, politically-correct apologising is an insult to proper historical study and is not equipping our children with a balanced view. There are very few nations in the world with an unblemished past.

I would much rather countries used their rich cultures and histories to add value to tomorrow rather than sink in the vortex of the bitterness and often ignorant prejudice of yesterday.

CHAPTER 5

THE WORLD MOVES EAST

Britain is a country which has been formed from many peoples – and we are also an offshore island. Offshore from Europe but also connected to every continent with our inherent trading skills and our long history of great economic and military reach. From what I've seen, the rest of the world envies our political stability, our integrity and our open business attitude.

One of our greatest assets, the City of London, sits in the premier trading time zone between the ravenous markets of Asia and the capital-rich US. We are, and always have been, in prime position. This little island has always looked to far horizons.

We have a huge ally in the United States. Our future is linked to theirs since so much of our trading history and today's corporate Britain is meshed with US Inc. But a lot of their power is rooted in the old world of big protectionism. The real economic power in the world is shifting to Asia – how we both deal with that will define success for our grandchildren.

But the wonderful, historical independence of our business aspirations and the historical ties with our former empire, forged in the mutual sacrifice of blood and treasure in the name of freedom, is hobbled by the European Union. We are both in it and out of it. We bow to the regulations, and we have access to its 'common market' but, unfortunately, our ambiguous membership means that we are hostage to its diktat whether we like it or not. The rest of the world sees us as part of the protectionism and self-interest of this huge trading bloc, and it dilutes our innate ability, born of centuries, to trade anywhere in the world. Globalisation is our natural market. It was made for Britain. We don't fear it as so many other countries do. Indeed, we have embraced it willingly.

In the nineteenth century, Britain led the world. In the twentieth, it was America's turn. The twenty-first century belongs to Asia.

Underlying it, as never before, is the concept of globalisation: the process by which independent regional economies, societies and cultures have become integrated and interdependent through a global network of communication, transportation, migration, capital flows and trade.

There are three main pillars of globalisation – the sale of goods and services; trans-border capital flows; and the biggest migration of peoples the world has ever seen. It's on that tapestry that Britain has to weave a journey of success in order to maximise its potential in the twenty-first century.

***

Let's look at the sale of goods and services around the world first. The days of selling things on price alone are over for the developed world – the UK, America, Japan, Canada, Australia, Germany and France all face this same problem. The developed world can no longer make its living by manufacturing something which merely sells because it's cheaper.

The only way forward for a developed economy is to capitalise on its cleverness and ingenuity. Millions of workers around the world do mass production much more cheaply than the mature economies. We must gear-change manufacturing process or provision of services into innovation, brand and quality, so that the product is not just a commodity whose price is determined simply by the market, but a product which has its own unique added value.

If we define innovation as taking an idea to market, making money out of invention or inventiveness, then the developed world has a ready-made route to escaping the race to the bottom of commodity manufacture.

Added value implies skills and education. Unless we skill our people, we don't have the knowledge to give a product or a system its unique saleable quality and its competitive edge.

There is another, politically seductive but ultimately ruinous alternative to all this – beggar-thy-neighbour protectionism. It soon descends into a self-destructive fight, and keeps the workforce living in the past and eventually sends them to the scrap heap. And out of protectionism can easily flow the dangerous, poisoned waters of nationalism and we all know where, at times of economic hardship and insecurity, that can lead. Free trade can be painful, particularly for an unskilled workforce, in the short term. 'Vote for me and I'll make you redundant' has never been a successful election-winning slogan! But with its inbuilt competition, drive for productivity enhancement (and thus greater profits and so larger tax revenues), its impetus to research and development (and thus a greater stimulus for the education system) and the opportunity to tap into markets which grow wider, deeper, richer and more capable of buying value-added goods and services every day, the reward for free trade is a safer, healthier, more integrated and more prosperous world. Countries which are mutually dependent on international trade tend not to fall out with each other.

One of the main, developed world culprits of protectionism is, ironically enough, the country which would most like to think of itself as a global free-trader, the United States. For example, in 2004, President George W Bush had a problem. American steel companies had not reformed their old unproductive ways, unlike Corus in the UK, which had been compelled to do so by the open market. The Americans were faced with two sorts of imports. One was cheap ordinary steel from China, South Korea and India, which was threatening to put the American steel mills out of business, and then specialist steels from the likes of the UK, Luxembourg, Germany and Sweden. At both levels American steel mills were losing out to imports in a major way.

So Bush announced a tariff on steel imports. It was pure protectionism, but it was dressed up as a measure to give the American steel mills time to modernise, to become more productive and more efficient.

Behind the political front was a thin excuse, which was to defend American steel mills from 'dumping' – where foreign countries subsidise their own steel industries so that they can sell at artificially reduced prices, destroy the steel industry in the country to which they are exporting and then ramp up their own prices again in what has become a near-monopoly market. There was evidence of this at the time, but using a politically populist sledge-hammer to crack a complicated nut was not the way to go.

Britain felt this insensitive commercial bullying particularly acutely. I remember at the CBI receiving a letter from a steel-worker in Rotherham in Yorkshire who said he was about to lose his job because of the inability of his employer to sell the speciality steel he made into the US market because of the new tariff. Yet his son was fighting shoulder-to-shoulder with the Americans in Iraq. Some way to treat your friends!

Bush's tariff was in breach of the World Trade Organisation rules, and there was an initial ruling against the US – Bush prevaricated, and then the European Union justified its existence, bringing clout that no individual member state could have delivered.

Its 520 million consumers happen to like orange juice, which was imported mostly from Brazil and Florida. So it was made very clear to the US that if they continued with the steel tariff, then the EU might not allow the import of Florida orange juice. Bush had had his own political problems in the Sunshine State at election time and didn't need to alienate the voters.

Sure enough, Bush gave way. He cloaked the climbdown by saying that, in his estimation, his steel mills had had enough time to become productive, and the tariff had only been a temporary measure. Really? The tariff was withdrawn, nothing changed.

The long term effect of protectionism is to embed the workforce in the past. Why train? Why become more competitive? Why advance?

The world has moved on, taking the need for higher skill levels with it. When the company goes bust the steel worker becomes just another unemployed, unskilled statistic, because an artificial price was his only protection. The challenge of the developed world is to skill up, so that employees are part of the value-added process, selling innovative products back to a China which is getting richer, instead of barricading itself against commodities which Asia will always produce more cheaply.

The long term effect of protectionism is to embed the workforce in the past. Why train? Why become more competitive? Why advance?

The whole concept of globalised goods and services which constantly improve and need ongoing investment in skills must take root because, every day, China is moving its 'wealth line' westwards from Eastern China, and the country is commoditising innovation all the time. As China's wealth line moves west the vacuum left behind is being filled with innovative and value-added products which they are assembling and producing themselves – not just commodities which compete on price, but high-end products which can be turned out in great volume. We need to keep pushing our skills level ever higher to enable production of more knowledge-based branded goods.

Of course, the constant dynamic of letting go yesterday's jobs carries the risk of the inherent destruction of communities that has led to so much of the damaging social dislocation in developed economies. Protectionism is not the answer, but a scared public urged on by vote-hungry politicians needs more easily understandable solutions than just 'free trade is a good thing in the long term'.

Our changing world brings new opportunities to challenged, developed economies. Sustainable energy generation in all its forms calls for innovation and skills that could not have been dreamt of a generation ago. An energy-hungry Asia will need to burn fossil fuels in ever-increasing quantities for generations to come. The challenge of how to facilitate that demand, in a way that doesn't pollute their communities or add to global warming, creates some wonderful opportunities for the changing, and hopefully improving, skills base of the developed world.

The internet has opened up routes to markets for small businesses that, to my mum and dad, would have seemed the stuff of HG Wells. And just as Britain's market place got a whole lot bigger, so the consequential getting-wealthier domestic markets of China and India, Brazil and Malaysia, Russia and Indonesia have become attractive to the developing world's manufacturers themselves, but sadly with all the latent protectionism that that awakes. Bangladesh and Vietnam are two examples of Asia's developing economies that receive deplorable protectionist treatment from some developing nations far more so than from those countries in the developed world.

***

The second pillar of globalisation is the trans-border flow of capital – the movement of money around the world, sometimes by governments but usually by banks, investors and businesses who operate in different countries, and in different currencies, often playing one off against the other. Personal debt, corporate debt and sovereign debt are all changing the way countries are able to govern.

Some countries are the weaker because of it, like Greece, which is paying the cost of its overseas investors panicking at the size of its national debt and its reluctance to restructure its economy; or African countries that allow such huge capital investment which makes them vulnerable to undue influence.

But the flow of capital also provides opportunities. Britain is the second biggest destination for inward investment in the world after America. It's not all money coming into the City being turned, churned, exchanged and then going out again. It's India's Tata buying Jaguar and Land Rover, it's Germany's BMW investing in the Mini in Oxford or Rolls Royce cars in Good-wood, it's the massive investments that the Saudis are making in chemicals and oil-derivative products on Teeside.

The other huge area which brings great benefit to the UK from the result of global capital flows is the City of London. It is still, but only just, the world's number one financial centre, despite all the problems of the last three years. Even after the financial crisis, the City of London can still legitimately say that if you want to invest your money or raise capital, if you want quality financial and legal advice, do it in the most amenable time zone and have the protection of doing it in a place where the rule of law means that you have an easily enforceable contract – then come to London. Its success is pivotal to the UK economy, generating nearly 13% of the country's direct and indirect tax revenues. Consider VAT, capital taxes and stamp duty paid by employees, and add income tax, corporation tax, bonus tax, and banking levy. It is clear to see that the tax generation by our banks, lawyers, accountants and insurers sure does pay down a key share of the deficit.

Whilst the banks must discharge their obligations to society more sustainably, sensitively, diligently and responsibly, if we make life so difficult for them that they leave these shores for good it would be the biggest own goal of all time. The knock-on blow to morale and the inability to attract skilled people from other lands to come to the UK to create wealth would be devastating for Britain. Socialists may say 'good riddance', and we all have a banker story that makes our blood boil, but their taxes pay a lot of teachers' wages and build a lot of hospitals.

But London's pre-eminence is being lost by the day as talent leaves for other financial centres, taking their taxes with them. 'We bailed them out' is an oft-heard cry. We did in a few cases, but our taxes did not rescue HSBC, Standard Chartered or Barclays. If they took their headquarters away from London it would be catastrophic for our country. Forcing unilateral regulation on them in Britain would render them unable to compete for the best talent in key emerging markets around the globe. To stay in business internationally they would have to leave ... and take their tax pounds with them.

It's not an empty threat that the banks may leave. Their operations wouldn't quit London altogether, but the real power and main taxpaying base lies where the headquarters are, and if these moved then that would a be huge and lasting loss to the City's prestige.

The banks' conduct has shown they need more relevant and better-enforced regulation, not simply more of it and certainly not so much more of it that either London is unfairly hit – to the benefit of other European capitals – or the UK becomes so uncompetitive in a globalised economy that Mumbai or Qatar, Dubai or Sao Paulo, Hong Kong or New York can't stop smiling.

***

The City's open attitude to the changed world of a globalised economy is a good example of the third pillar of globalisation; migration.

For over a thousand years, the UK and its constituent parts have been open to people coming from other countries with their skills and their talent, making money for themselves in a secure liberal environment, adding value to the nation, paying some tax and building a more prosperous country.

Look at Courtaulds – a good old British textile manufacturer. British? No. Monsieur Courtauld was a French Huguenot, who came here in the seventeenth century after his home country had said that if he were to continue to worship his god in the way he did, then he and his family would meet a rather nasty end. He eventually settled in Lincoln and the rest is history.

When the Siemens brothers had an idea about electronic switch-gear and wanted to raise capital, before World War I, the place to come to was London. There was a ready- made legal framework to protect the intellectual property of their idea, there was an open, tolerant society, there was a reliable, enforceable system for raising money and a place where they could freely make their product and then sell it round the world, because Britain was such a global clearing house for money and manufacture.

And really it ought to be the same today, all these years on, if our country is to succeed. We need a young person coming out of a university in Bangalore to choose, like millions before him from all over the world, to ply his trade in the City of London, make some money, pay some tax and do it in Britain. But sadly he won't be able to under the Coalition government's current immigration policy.

We, the nation of immigrants long before Columbus discovered America, have introduced a cap on non-EU migration. So if you are, for example, a New Zealand entrepreneur with a great idea – just like those Siemens brothers but a hundred years on – and you want to come to London, raise some capital, protect your idea and make it in Britain, you won't be able to. It's entirely likely that your grandfather was of the New Zealand generation who travelled 10,000 miles, fought his way up a beach and died so that the British aren't speaking German today, but that makes no difference. The meaningful historical links so many of us have in one way or another with India, Canada, the Caribbean, Australia or New Zealand count for nothing. With 2500 men from India dying at El Alamein and men from the West Indies falling on the Normandy beaches the young people in many of our immigrant communities should wear the poppy with pride. Their forefathers bought this generation's freedom by paying the ultimate price just as mine did.

Up to April 2011 only 24,100 people will be allowed in from outside the EU to work, 5% less than came in during the year of serious economic recession, 2008/09. A third of the academic teachers at our top universities come from outside the EU. At our universities there are 75,000 undergraduates and postgraduates from non-EU countries, each paying three times the fees of a student from the EU. We need to be internationally competitive by attracting the best talent in the world not just from a group of 27 countries, many of them post-growth.

We signed up to a European Union with a set of rules which enshrine free movement of labour, those who just want to come and live in Britain from Latvia or Lithuania are able to settle here whether or not they have a job. They are so very welcome if they are prepared to contribute and integrate, those Polish workers in the Peterhead docks being a great example, but we are turning away people who will speak English, integrate into society, create wealth for themselves and wealth for the country, just because they don't come from the EU. Our history as a trading nation has made us very conscious of other skills around the world. Let's encourage them, if they want to come here. We already live in a country where one in three households depend on the state for half their income. We cannot afford any increase in welfare dependency and we certainly won't fix Britain if our public services are swamped by an influx of people who don't contribute to our economy by getting a worthwhile job.

It is a time for leadership, it is a time to say that we are changing the rules on immigration. On our own if necessary.

We have a track record of welcoming people from abroad from the humblest persecuted trader up to our various Royal Families. How does it help Britain to say to Australia, Canada, New Zealand or India, sorry, regardless of how skilled you are, you can't come because we have a cap on immigration? The damage to UK business and to our standing in the globalised economy will be enormous. Uncle Sam is having to learn, with some difficulty, that globalisation is not Americanisation; British business must not let the European Union fall foul of the same issue.

It is a time for leadership, it is a time to say that we are changing the rules on immigration. On our own if necessary.

If we don't deal with the immigration side of the three pillars of globalisation, then the other two – in which we excel –will be wasted.

***

Globalisation means a huge shift in the balance of economic power, and Britain needs to move with it. This is Asia's century, but the former head of the top table is still there. America is still vitally important to us, since she is our single biggest trading partner in the world, and every day two and a half million people in the US go to work for companies which are headquartered in Britain – and for their part two million of us work here in the UK for companies which have their base in the United States.

So we have a vested interest in America's ability to face up to its rivals in the world league.

In particular, China. In 2010 the country was officially recognised as the second largest economy in the world, having surged ahead from being the seventh largest only ten years ago. The smart money is on her becoming the largest economy on the planet by 2020, displacing the United States.

In a clear demonstration of the very significant shift in power, for the first time ever, it was China and the other major developing economies – Brazil, India and South Korea – which led the world out of the global economic slowdown. In fact, if it hadn't been for them, we in the mature markets would still be deep in the mire. According to the World Bank, by 2050, China and India will together account for nearly 50% of global GDP – equivalent to the output of all of today's G7 countries.

These and other emerging economies all have vital characteristics which mark them out as fit for purpose in the globalisation race that is the twenty-first century – high savings rates, skilled, hard working people, innovative strategies for growth and large, getting-richer domestic markets.

What a contrast to the 'mature' economies like Europe and the US, with their weak domestic demand, overcapacity, stubbornly high unemployment with high wage costs and a greater disinclination to put in the hours (indeed, in an EU mired in the Working Time Directive, the actual criminalisation of putting in the hours), more expensive borrowing, benefit-ready governments which take the responsibility of skilling-up away from the workforce – and, most importantly, increased protectionism on a beggar-thy-neighbour road to another downturn.

America is still in the chair at the top table, but she, like all the mature economies, will need to revise her table manners towards the new seating arrangements. The rude awakening over the biggest and nastiest recession for 75 years should have set out the harsh reality for every American citizen. The US will need to open its trade borders even wider to the next New World, and to understand that it, too, needs to reform its old-fashioned industries, but more importantly, recognise that its days as the only number one are numbered. A constructive relationship between the leaders of the twentieth century and the new leaders of the twenty-first will be the major challenge for political and business leaders in the coming years. It could just be one of the defining components of a century of prosperity and security, or not.

The UK and US have history of course. But the 'special relationship' has often been one way. President Roosevelt told Winston Churchill quite openly and correctly, that American intervention

American 'aid' came at a huge cost to her best friend. The UK only finished paying off its war loans, with interest, in 2008. in World War II was not to save the British Empire. So, as many a British possession in various spheres of influence around the world found, in 1946, they now had a new quasi-colonial master.

American 'aid' came at a huge cost to her best friend. The UK only finished paying off its US war loans, with interest, in 2008.

That isn't to say that the Americans have not been generous around the world. If it hadn't been for their countless sacrifices then we would never have defeated the forces of fascism, so I acknowledge fully the price that America has paid for being number one. But she is going to have to get used to the fact that the world has changed forever. China, India, Russia, Brazil, and many of the Middle East states will come to the top table in one way or another. And I wonder whether or not there will there be room for both little Britain and little France on a future Security Council, while a rapidly growing, nuclear armed India, with her billion people as a fully paid-up member of the new world order, is excluded from it.

How America gets used to that new balance will define its place in the twenty-first century. It is also still living in the past as far as its domestic industrial policy is being applied. In 2009, its biggest carmaker, General Motors, filed for Chapter 11 bankruptcy. It had been unproductively making cars that fewer people wanted to buy, but in the end the US Treasury ended up part-owning the Motown company to the tune of $57.6 billion.

It is almost beyond belief that a government in this new world of value-added innovation should wish to keep a GM alive, especially a government of a country that considers itself the last great protector of the raw meat of free markets and capitalism. Some double standard. We have a couple of words to define that in Britain and they are 'British Leyland'. It took from 1975 to 2005 for a British Prime Minister to have the courage to let it go. Harold Wilson put the money in, Callaghan and Thatcher added to it but finally Blair had enough confidence in the fundamental structural change which was happening in the UK and, importantly, the British people's unspoken acknowledgement of that, that he let it go into receivership, and in the middle of a General Election campaign as well; that's how far the UK had travelled in adapting to a changed world.

General Motors has now been reintroduced to the private sector by way of flotation on the stock market. It has been nursed back to health through nationalisation ... in America! But it will never be the same again. About 16% of what was once the world's largest company is now held by Asia and the Middle East's sovereign wealth funds. I wonder if the average American on Main Street USA realises that 1% of The General is held by SAIC the Shanghai automotive manufacturer located in what is now the world's biggest market for cars … China. That's the reality of globalisation.

How America deals with these main issues of sale of goods and services, capital flows and migration, is going to define the country's success or failure in Asia's century. The US is a 300 million strong market of people who quite like buying British goods and services. Given our close links, the more open the American market is, the more attuned globally America is, the better it is for Britain.

***

In 1945, if you had drawn a longitudinal line to show the point of economic balance in the world, on one side the might of America and on the other a world debilitated by World War Two, it would have been about 30 miles off New York. Move on to 1990, I guess that line might have been down the Rhine or the Danube and Western Europe and America would have been moved together to balance the rest of the world. Today that line has achieved a place where it's going to stay for a hundred years, and that's straight down the Gulf – which is going to be the hub of the world.

Aviation is a sector that has to take the long view and its investment plans now all centre on the Gulf as a hub. Aircraft purchases for ten years hence indicate that the Atlantic will become a bus stop service – the big planes and the big traffic will be going to Asia. And they want to put their planes down in Dubai, or Abu Dhabi or Bahrain.

What's important to us is that Britain has excellent relations with the Gulf States. They like us, they like coming to London, they like investing in our country. We constantly need to nurture that relationship.

In order to do that, we need to change the mood music. We need to understand how hard the nations of the Middle East are working to develop alternatives to fossil fuels, for example. They have every interest in keeping consumption of fossil fuels going, but they are developing peaceful nuclear energy, and other forms of sustainable energy. They are working on driving carbon out of the use of oil and gas. They are building up manufacturing bases and centres of training and knowledge transfer. Britain, through its businesses and its universities, has shown itself to be on tomorrow's page. It's time for more and more cooperation with the Gulf States, a real win–win.

***

Another significant high table member will be India. A billion people and the country has barely started to industrialise yet. As they grow, they will begin to pollute the planet in an unprecedented way. One Indian minister I met in my trade minister

Another significant high table member will be India. A billion people and the country has barely started to industrialise yet. days said that he was not going to curb the economic growth of India with environmental legislation when the developed industrial nations had been growing and polluting for the past 200 years. So how India can industrialise in a greener way is an enormous challenge, not just for India, but everyone on our planet.

But for Britain there's tremendous potential in our relationship with India. She is a relatively tolerant society. They really 'get' education. The family is the central core, and they travel well. They go round the world, they integrate into society. Their children do their homework, pass their exams and create wealth.

Britain starts ahead of the game with India. We have 1.3 million non-resident Indians in the UK who are studying, working and creating jobs and taxable wealth. They are very welcome and we should encourage more into an integrated society here. If ever a cap on immigration was to prove an own goal for UK business, this is it.

At the same time, India quite correctly doesn't see us as having any special rights in trade and investment – nor should we expect it. We are but one of many countries beating a path to their door and I applaud David Cameron's huge trade and investment initiative with India which ought to be the start of a step change in dealings between our two countries.

We also understand each other, in another, much more 'family' way. In fact we might say we're ahead of the game, since neither the French, nor the Americans, the Japanese, the Germans, the Brazilians nor the Russians play cricket. That sounds trivial but the universality of sport is a great help for international relations, and there is that natural bond between us.

We must continue to welcome them to our shores, but also remind them that it's a two way street. Why can't more banking licences be granted to the HSBCs, the Barclays and the Standard Chartereds of this world? They can offer micro-finance facilities in rural India, which is something the protected Indian Banks are reluctant to do as there is no competitive spur to make them. They may be doing more now, but it is nowhere near what could be achieved with the spur of outside competition. What's wrong with a Tesco or a Sainsbury's in their towns and cities? If our top flight legal companies could operate in India, added value for the Indian economy would follow. These are our value-added goods and services and we are good at them. But so far the protectionist doors are firmly closed. And of course India is a democracy with as many vested interests as any other. We need to understand what their issues are. Change will be gradual, but we need to be bargaining for Britain at the table of trade every day.

India wants an opening into European markets for its agricultural products, but the French and other southern Mediterranean members of the EU are standing in the way. We, as members of the European Union, are caught by that because we are in the same trading bloc. When I was a minister I found that so frustrating. Our natural inclination is to allow our economy to experience Indian produce and in return get more UK banks trading in India. This two-way flow is thwarted by the protectionist attitudes of Southern European members of the EU who don't want India entering into their agricultural markets as competition.

***

With that sort of issue at stake – a one billion-strong developing nation hungry for business and knocking at the door of a subsidised, self-interested agglomeration of 27 states flying together in very loose formation, with no destination in view apart from a return to the 1970s – I think it's time for some change.

The EU is currently not fit for the globalisation challenges ahead, which we need to meet successfully for our survival and prosperity. There is so much going for 520 million sophisticated consumers living in democratic peace as they face the challenges of the next decades. But retiring inwardly from the global race and not tooling up for the fight in the hope we can go on paying ourselves money we've never earned derived from businesses we have rendered uncompetitive is not a winning strategy!

When I was at the CBI, we used to sit down with an organisation called UNICE – Union National Industriel et Commercial

Européan, now known as Business Europe, which is the umbrella organisation for the equivalents of the CBI in the European Union member countries. Our job was to decide on the issues upon which we'd lobby Brussels on behalf of our members.

We began to talk about a key issue – patent protection. It's extremely expensive to file a patent in the EU, partly because it has to be translated and distributed in over 20 languages – including those two global business languages, Welsh and Gaelic!

UNICE was beginning to say that it might be a good idea to have the patent protection in one language, because it would be cheaper and more efficient, and patents are the lifeblood of innovation, enterprise and a knowledge-based economy.

The Germans, the Spanish and the Italians proposed that the language of the patents should be the global language of business, English. But the French representative stood up and said he agreed that there should be one language, but that language had to be French.

Now if you think about how many countries speak English as their first language and then add to that the number who speak it as a second language – the total of English speakers is in the billions, especially in those parts of the world where we must go and develop our markets. Whereas only a hundred million or so at most speak French as a first or second language.

But as soon as the French delegation demanded their own language, the Germans, the Spanish and the Italians changed their minds as well in favour of their own country's tongue. We were back to square one. It seemed to me those abortive talks were a mirror of most of EU decision making.

It's impossible to formulate a competitive Europe with that kind of divisive national interest. In 2000, the leaders of the EU met in Lisbon and created the Lisbon Agenda. Tony Blair, Gerhard Schroder and the rest pledged to make Europe the most competitive place to do business in the world by 2010.

I was at a conference in Oxford, (as a rookie DG), where Blair and Schroder were speaking the day after the fanfare announcement of this new 'Agenda for Business'. I asked them when they would start creating laws to make us more competitive, rather than just talking about it. They said that every year they would test the Agenda's progress against law-making and regulatory enforcement in various EU member states. I said I doubted it. The disapproval of the EU elite in the room was palpable – they were the talkers rather than the doers. I felt the presence of a small businessman from Yorkshire on my shoulder who had told me he'd believe it when he saw less regulation, uniform regulatory enforcement in all EU countries, less protectionism and globally competitive government engagement, not an EU still wrapped up in social planning, labour market suffocation, environmental policy supremacy and the sacred cow of the taxpayer subsidising the Common Agricultural Policy. My Yorkshireman was proved right. In three years Iraq became the main issue and the Lisbon Agenda and its competitive promises quietly disappeared.

> **The EU was born out of the best of intentions: to achieve economic growth in a peaceful environment.**

The EU was born out of the best of intentions: to achieve economic growth in a peaceful environment after the ruins of World War II. Firstly, to create a single market in coal and steel without tariffs and without restraint. Implicit in the union was the thought that the Germans would work hard to repair their country and the French knowing that the closer you hug a foreign enemy the harder it is for them to stab you again, did just that. They did of course want to run the whole thing as well. Belgium, Holland, Luxembourg and Italy came along for the ride. That was 1957, under the Treaty of Rome. With typical British aloofness and the justifiable fact that we had a commonwealth providing a huge 'domestic' market, the UK stayed out and, by the time we woke up, it was too late.

So, in 1973, our then Prime Minister Edward Heath, who'd had personal experience of World War II and its degradation of people and nations, saw this union as a positive opportunity to avoid it ever happening again. He was presiding over the basket case of an economy that the UK had become. He knocked on the door of entry to the club one more time. He had very few bargaining chips to play with. The price of entry, then and now, was and is very high.

The greatest EU success is peace. We have been through almost 70 years, during which time the 27 members of the European Union have not fought each other. An historical first. Most of the founder members of the EU think of it as a union for peace first and foremost. And there's certainly nothing wrong with that.

But the people of Britain, without the wartime experience of being occupied, sees it primarily as a market, a union for trade. That's how Edward Heath sold it to the British public and that's what it was going to be. A common market. What we have instead is this enormous drive for federalism – sometimes openly promoted, often subliminally advanced – not for a common market but for a common central government with some powers left at national level. The French liked it because it meant that they could run Europe while the Germans could rebuild their broken nation on wealth creation and hard work, and banish the damaging na-tionalism of the past. Unfortunately along came Britain with a very different view of the EU – we saw it as a free trade area, and not the beginnings of a new European country.

Europe is schismatic. It isn't one country at all, nor can it ever be. There is no single community of purpose.

Britain entered on the basis of trade. We were never 'up' for a united Europe and would never have voted for one given the chance. Germany had been at the gates of Paris three times in

a century; the French and the Germans were rightly resolved that must never happen again. A big
achievement was the entry of the former Soviet Union satellite countries that could have easily fallen
into failed state status right in our backyard. The EU
was a ready-made haven of democratic capitalism
for them. What a win–win that was for us all, in so
many ways.

... along came Britain with a very different view of the EU – we saw it as a free trade area, and not the beginnings of a new European country.

But what the long-term effect of these newish entrants will be is difficult to predict. Romania and Bulgaria for
example, were not ready for entry. Greece cut corners in order
to make the Euro-entry requirements, and has now paid a heavy
price. Poland, which weathered the recession better than many
of the larger economies, UK included, has 40 million people,
almost the size of Spain. A major player, but with a long, expensive way to go to catch up. The new entrants can become great,
getting-wealthier markets for UK business or they can turn into
a drag anchor on the major EU economies ... the challenge is
there for sure. Quite how much political sovereignty has Ireland
surrendered in taking German bailout funds? Can you have
monetary union in bad times without some form of fiscal or political union? Will the German voter reward action taken in the
name of European security and stability with defeat at the polls
for their leader? The rules of the game are changing almost by
the day. Where will that leave European business competitiveness in Asia's century?

So we've ended up with a European Union in the second decade of the new century, which is not fit for the race that is globalisation. And because we are affected so much by its bloc thinking, a large spanner gets thrown into the work of fixing Britain.

It has also failed its first real test. When economies are going forward you can paper over the cracks and borrow your way out of trouble, with growing receipts coming into treasuries. The moment the pressure comes on, deficits appear, countries go into recession – and as one of the world's greatest investors, Warren Buffet, put it, 'when the tide goes out it shows the wrecks at the bottom of the sea'.

And so it was with Greece – a country that marches to the beat of a different drum – the gentle tones of the bouzouki can't disguise the harsh reality of enormous debts, the contingent debt of pension provision which stretches out over the next few decades; yet there's enormous government spending, and corruption, whilst tax paying is virtually a voluntary event.

Look at Hellenic Railways. Recently, some reports put its losses at around one billion Euros a year on revenues of two hundred million! An annual deficit of five times its turnover. Its indebtedness has possibly reached 5% of the GDP of Greece! A Greek train driver's salary could reach €120,000. Greece knows that they can get away with it because in the last resort and when all the fine speeches have been made 'Europe' will bail them out. So a German car worker sees his retirement age go up to 67 to pay for a Greek train driver retiring at 55.

This adds to the schisms in the whole system. Imagine you're working on the Volkswagen production line in Wolfsburg. You've been brought up at your grandmother's knee, with very stern advice concerning financial rectitude and saving, about never again allowing inflation in your economy because great grandfather told you what happened in the Weimar Republic. You'll be taking a pretty dim view of your fellow European Unionists in Greece, especially since you've also been brought up to believe in the merits of hard work. Now some of the tax taken from your hard work is going to be paying for the financial sins of others in the name of a united Europe. They haven't bothered to play by the rules of your Union and your money is going to bail them out.

With its corporatist, highly regulated approach, Brussels spent a decade of ignoring global competitiveness and instead it's been trying to build a social Europe. Inward looking, it has forgotten that the European Union has to compete in a century which belongs to Asia. The whole European project has been marching valiantly back towards the 1970s. In the globalisation race it matters not a jot that Spain is equal to Sweden, or Italy to Ireland; we have 520 million people living in sustainable peace for the first time ever and to exploit that for the benefit of everyone we must provide businesses with a value-added reason to belong.

Britain is part of it. The EU spends more of our taxes on the Common Agricultural Policy than on universities, research and development and education. How can that render twenty-first century Europe fit for purpose? Where is the future economic growth going to develop? In the production of commodities whose price is determined by anyone but the producer, or in the hotbeds of research and learning in an innovative, twenty-first century Europe? The EU must move away from the domination of agriculture. Up until recently, each European cow received a daily subsidy of about $2, which is twice what a third of the world's population scrapes by on each day.

One issue that surfaced when I was at the CBI showed an ideological hypocrisy in Brussels. On the one hand banning tobacco advertising, including on the much-publicised and globally recognisable speedy billboards of Formula One, and on the other using EU taxpayers' money, through the CAP, to subsidise the growing of tobacco in Greece, Spain, Italy and even Germany. Some of it was cropped and then burnt on the roadside because it was of insufficient quality with which to make a cigarette. I raised the matter several times in Brussels but the vested governmental interests had their way and the long march backwards continued. The attitude seemed to be one of 'let it happen and it will change over time' yet the British people, and British business in particular, would have been livid if they'd known. The sheer waste of money in the years before so-called change could take place is inexcusable.

I mentioned earlier the raft of employment legislation which Tony Blair and Labour adopted in 1997 on our behalf as the Social Chapter. We are fighting our global competitors with rules that are intended to make Europeans work less hard.

If you imagine globalisation as a race, the European Union entrant is 27 countries tied together at the leg.

If you imagine globalisation as a race, the European Union entrant is 27 countries tied together at the leg. When one country has a broken leg, which renders it less competitive, rather than using its collective strength to mend the broken limb, the EU tries hard to ensure every member gets a broken leg as well! Using member states' collective talent to push up to a best-in-class standard ... now that would be the EU at its finest, not dumbing down to find the lowest common denominator.

We're all limping along with the same disability – the Working Time Directive, the Agency Temps Directive or other labour market legislation. We're out of the race before it starts – all on the losing side together. So everyone can have prizes, we're all the same; we have achieved a common market and relegated ourselves to the rear of the globalisation race. Brussels passes laws banning people from working more than 48 hours a week, even if they want to, and politicians talk about competing with Asia ... it's laughable, or would be if it wasn't so serious.

Britain has fought long and hard to keep itself away from labour market legislation which slows us down in the race for global competitiveness. But, bit by bit, we're seeing that eroded. They're breaking our leg to make us the same as those with the broken legs – the high unemployment of crippled labour markets elsewhere in social Europe. But it could be worse. At least we didn't go into the Euro during the days of the financial crisis. I often thought of those endless 'shall we/shan't we' debates about Euro entry back in 2000. Our independence and our ability to set our own interest rates, print our own money (for that is what quantitive easing really is), take advantage in overseas markets of a weaker currency, and carry all that out at a timing of our choice, has, frankly, saved London from being the Athens of the next decade.

I know it is not fashionable to do so, but credit should be given where it's due. Giving independence to the Bank of England, keeping the UK out of the Euro in the teeth of a campaign to the contrary from his next-door neighbour in Downing Street, and corralling the major economic powers into coordinated support of the international banking system at a time of acute crisis, were all achievements of Gordon Brown. Many were his faults and mistakes but I shudder to think where our country's financial system would be now if Mr Brown had called those big three decisions differently.

***

The much talked-about possible accession of Turkey is of great importance to the EU of the future. Britain has always loved exploiting getting-richer new markets and Turkey would be a highly successful EU partner for the UK. It is a moderate Muslim but secular state. If Europe doesn't take it into the fold, it could fall victim to fundamentalism, and that would be a sinister threat to Europe's flank, let alone to the constitutionally free people of Turkey. Through the Bosphorus come some 55,000 ship movements a year with a lot of the oil and gas that the West needs. I would prefer it if that bottleneck were under the control of people who are friendly to us and part of the club of democratic capitalism.

So it would suit our security to have Turkey as part of the Union. Turkey has also made huge efforts to bring itself into line with the entry qualifications for the EU. The French and the Germans are saying no, because they don't want a Muslim country in what they feel should be essentially a Christian constituency. The immigration card is being played blatantly with a populist agenda.

That is racism. Turkey would be a huge and important part of the Union, a 75 million strong nation, increasing the EU's economic performance over time. Turkey's economy is growing at 5% pa unlike the EU average of 1.7%. Turkish entrepreneurs in the EU today employ half a million people and run €40 billion worth of businesses. According to the OECD Turkey would, by 2050, be the second largest economy in the EU, capable of pulling other member states out of cyclical downturns.

Turkey is such a large, efficient manufacturer and, as its population got richer, they would, with a single tariff-free market, start to buy our value-added goods and services – everyone wins. The US has shown that competitive exporting is easier off the base of a large domestic market. Turkey would add to the EU's advantage here in short order. We need Turkey inside and not outside the tent. And the spectre of EU-wide migration, which rightfully worries the more developed economies especially at times of austerity and high domestic unemployment, can be dealt with by simply changing the EU rules governing rights of entry. We would emerge with a huge, powerful, tariff-free trading area concentrating on competitive Business Europe not a Social Europe of broken legs, hobbling along at the back of the field in the globalisation stakes.

The accession of a secular but culturally different nation to the EU would force reform, halting the path to federalism and give the EU a wider, deeper market. We would all be better off for Turkey's membership of the EU – and not just financially.

∗∗∗

It's time for businesses to get tough. Germany has world beating skills in engineering and infrastructure building. It has again become the engine of Europe, and is one of the world's biggest exporters. France has a skills improvement culture to be envied. Why don't we – alongside these two powerful members with their globally recognised accomplishments – bring pressure on Brussels to impose legislation improving skills and value-added businesses, shifting the aid from commodities to knowledge transfer rather than dumbing down regulations which will eventually consign the European workforce to an industrial anachronism?

And if Brussels won't do it, then it's time for UK business to use its globalised open market credentials to ask some very big questions of those who make the rules – see global competitiveness coming from the business-friendly implementation of rules they make, or ask, where is the added value in being in the club and not just an associate member? European politicians and officials have to realise just how serious this is. Some of our biggest companies are sending their head offices abroad for tax reasons. Some are threatening to go because they're smothered in politically motivated legislation. Other businesses might say that they'll do the same because Brussels stifles their flair. They could go to Turkey, Vietnam, Mexico, Brazil or, of course, India or China, and many other countries who would be hungry for their inward investment and taxes, and would, without doubt, put an able and willing workforce at their disposal. We can't fix Britain if Brussels continues to break our leg, hindering our progress in the global race.

If we don't want to lose our talented, agile companies, then we need to alter the way we implement European legislation. Britain is quite well behaved about playing it by the rules – implementing legislation at enormous cost to businesses when often other countries hardly bother.

Our worst enemy is ourselves. The civil service in Britain for many years thought that it was their bounden duty to gold plate every piece of EU-inspired legislation. Instead of making the rules more workable, they applied and enforced them as if business was the enemy rather than the partner. Traffic wardens do that. Our public servants should have a smart and comprehensive handle on legislation which they know is being imposed from elsewhere, so it works *with* the grain of business, not against it. That's what officials from other competitor member states do. We in the UK have a history of individuality. Why don't we all attempt to water down the influx of Brussels bureaucracy, or take a more circumspect view of the rules – especially at the level of governmental enforcement? Others do – frequently. If we don't, then our competitive advantage is shot, because businesses have a choice in a globalised economy as to where they locate – and it won't be Britain. It will probably not be in the EU either, but that is hardly the point.

Overnight we could change that. Let us act in our own interests. We will do it in exactly the same way others do.

I have been told for many years that you can't seek compliance by others if you don't comply yourself, that reform is a long process, that it's all going in the right direction, that 'these things take time'. Well I am failing to see where the added-value for my country is in an EU that, in many ways, needs us more than we need them, an EU that takes every chance to reduce the competitiveness of our financial services sector, that still pays homage at the feet of the CAP, that has constantly failed to get a clean audit report.

And now, with the peoples of member states having faced the worst recession for a lifetime, with governments all over Europe cutting public services and increasing taxes, Brussels forces through a 2.9% rise in its budget with the people of 27 belea-guered countries having to find €126.5 billion extra a year! No democratic connection to worry about. And still the farmers will get more than the universities: €43.7 billion being spent on the Common Agricultural Policy, with an additional €862 mil-lion funding a national support programme for the wine sector alone. As nations from Ireland to Italy are forced to cut, a futur-istic new headquarters for the European Council is being built in Brussels at a cost of €260 million. MEPs have doubled their entertainment budget. What's more, the entire European Par-liament moves once a month between Brussels and Strasbourg at the enormous cost of tens of millions of Euros, merely to as-suage French pride. We have no hope of fixing Britain and driv-ing through change, of promoting the undoubted benefits of the EU and taking advantage of them for the good of our country, if such alarming and misdirected spending does not stop now.

So let us take the lead on competitiveness, on promoting research and development instead of job-reducing legislation.

I think we would find a lot of new friends among the members of the EU. The member states have a wealth of highly skilled companies who produce world quality products. It defies the logic of business that these firms wouldn't do better if they were under a freer common market, and were unchained from the rules which threaten to march them back into the last century. Things must change. The EU we belong to must change. If not, then the question 'what does the EU give us that membership of a European Free Trade Area does not?' has no answer in the quest for a value-added, globally competitive, wealth creating, tariff-free business environment in Asia's century.

It is worth remembering which country now has the world's largest currency reserves, the world's largest vehicle market, which country is the largest trading partner of Brazil and India, is the world's largest exporter and the world's largest producer of steel … and greenhouse gases. Not the US. Not the European Union nor any one of its member states. Not Japan. It is, of course, China. It is how we in Britain, how the peoples of Europe, and those men and women – elected and unelected – who govern us, deal with this fact, that will define our success or failure in the decades ahead.

CHAPTER 6

THE BUSINESS OF POLITICS: FIXING THE SYSTEM

If Britain is going to become fit for purpose and be able to compete in a globalised century, there is an urgent need for major, far-reaching constitutional reform.

Our private sector has had to change its working practices or die, and big questions are being asked of the role, the funding and the delivery mechanisms of the public sector.

A similar reconstruction needs to be made to the way the country is run and the way in which its lawmakers, our MPs, are elected.

If government is going to ask so much more of the people of the country, if we truly are going to be 'all in this together' and go through stormy waters as one, then we should demand from those that govern our lives legitimacy, relevance, efficiency, competence and experienced skills.

We should be asking some fundamental questions. How should MPs be elected? Is the way we choose a Prime Minister compatible with the sentiment and true mindset of the people? Should there be a House of Lords and, if so, how should a second chamber be constituted?

The Coalition government breaks new ground every day, and yet public disillusionment with Members of Parliament and our political system has never been higher. There has never been a better time to bring about meaningful, radical change in our constitution and make the way we govern ourselves more relevant to twenty-first century Britain, making it fairer to those who live in it and more efficient in its delivery.

Then the country stands a chance of becoming fit for the battles of globalisation that lie ahead.

***

We have, first of all, too many Members of Parliament. When a constituency size was defined by the ability of an MP to do his rounds on horseback, and to get his message across on a soapbox in a town square or at a mass meeting in a town hall, the current number of MPs and the size of constituencies worked well.

There has never been a better time to bring about meaningful, radical change in our constitution and make the way we govern ourselves more relevant to twenty-first century Britain ...

The world is different today. The ways in which we communicate have changed forever and are in constant flux. We just do not need as many people to do the job; to those working in both the public and private sector that sounds very familiar. Why should MPs be immune from the world out there? The present government is committed to cutting the number from 650 to 600. That slight reduction has already caused a huge outbreak of political strife, as if war is being declared. I would suggest some real effective change for no more hassle, and slim the House of Commons down to 400, to serve our 60 million population. It can be done – India, for example manages to serve a democracy of a billion people with just 500 MPs.

That would mean fewer and larger constituencies but, of course, today's MPs are not on horseback. The laptop, the mobile phone, television and the internet – and all the social media – provide enough support and conduits to do the same job for many more people over a wider area. Voters' expectations have altered and, in a world where everything appears on a screen in one way or another, people need to feel more personally involved in

Westminster's decision-making process and the way our elected representatives work.

MPs must build on the better and more frequent use of technology and, as I argue later in this chapter, make use of the time freed up by being at Westminster less, by reinforcing personal involvement and understanding in their enlarged constituencies. However, this calls for the public to play its part as well; an MP's mailbox is full of correspondence, much of which is being directed to the wrong person. No MP will admit that much of this correspondence should go first to one of the myriad of different agencies. Voter alienation is not exactly a route for reelection, but we must all help improve the more efficient use of an MP's time by the people who pay their wages. We must get the message across by information campaigns at least, that we should be asking for an MP's help only after other primary channels have failed us.

The electorate will not worry about losing specific constituencies, whatever the opponents of reform may say. They don't now think of themselves as coming from, or relating to, the sort of area that the current official boundary defines. I'm sure that voters in the suburbs of Leeds, for example, don't feel themselves part of 'Leeds North-West', rather than Leeds itself.

Such change would not be before time. After all, one Member of Parliament can currently represent 55,000 people whilst another

THE BUSINESS OF POLITICS: FIXING THE SYSTEM

can encompass 70,000. But both these MPs have the same single vote in Parliament. This is hardly representative. Of course there would be obvious practical exceptions. For example the Isle of Wight is geographically and societally one constituency and common sense dictates that nothing should change there.

***

Numerical representation would average up, but it doesn't make the actual selection of Members of Parliament any more representative of everyone who lives in a new, enlarged constituency.

There are still 'safe' seats, where the twenty or so activists on the local party committee will select the candidate for a particular party without any formal reference to anyone else. In a constituency with a majority of over ten thousand which is big enough to withstand virtually any swing at election time, that candidate will be returned as the MP for tens of thousands of people who had no say in the selection process because their party, not the individual, is dominant.

For example, in Huntingdon, anyone standing in blue for election would be duly returned as the Conservative Member of Parliament. In Erdington, Birmingham, you could do the same with someone dressed in red and the Labour Party would almost certainly get one more seat at Westminster. Both would be chosen more often than not by a handful of party activists.

Attempts are being made to widen the approval and consultation process by many a constituency, and meetings of over a hundred are often used to create a short list. But, even then, the 'safe seat' existence hardly reflects the choice of the many.

In the General Election of 1959 the Conservative party formed a government with 58% of the seats at Westminster when only 49.7% of the popular vote went their way. In the 2005 Election Tony Blair stayed at Number 10 with the support of 55% of Commons seats when only 35.3% of the voters put a cross in a Labour box. These two examples show that the election process is unfair, unrepresentative and it must change.

One suggested solution is proportional representation, but in that system the candidate is chosen by the party's central organisation and the individual has no real connection with his or her local area. In effect, the party slate wins, and the local community loses any feeling that it has any say in the country's decision-making process at individual level. That is the antithesis of any notion of connected democracy.

No system is perfect and fault can be found in all. But, to my mind, the alternative vote system is better. Candidates who are the majority's second or third choice as stated on the ballot paper are considered for another chance if there is not a 50%-plus-one vote winner in the first count. At least it means that the elected

Member of Parliament has the general backing of over 50% of the constituency who voted.

Making voting compulsory would make the result even more relevant to the wishes of the electorate. There would need to be a box to enable the registration of abstentions, but so many more people would actually consider the choices and exercise their hard-won right to vote for someone.

It would take a few years to make this new voting system work, but I am asking for meaningful and lasting change. It has taken many years and many wars to try to make sure that we can all make decisions as equals. Change is never easy, but some growing pains would be worth it to achieve an electoral system which was a lot fairer, more relevant and, most importantly, allows more people to connect with the process.

***

People must feel their vote matters or they won't buy into the other big changes needed to fix Britain. The electorate today is used to much more immediate and relevant ways of voting for what they want – witness the fact that often more people vote for contestants in reality television programmes than vote for their preferred politicians in elections.

... often more people vote for contestants in reality television programmes than vote for their preferred politicians in elections.

To rid the system of the undemocratic charade, where a few activists send their preferred person to Westminster, or the parachuting of the party leadership's favourite into a safe seat, regardless of local opinion, we need to turn to the United States.

Their system of primaries at grass-roots level allows local voters to select their parliamentary candidate before he or she takes their chances in a general election.

The Conservatives trialled this before the 2010 General Election and it should become the norm. Our politicians need to work much harder to engage their voters and to convince them that they are truly representative, and that the individual is not being ignored by the party machine.

Public expectations have changed. We are no longer deferential to the political class. The expenses scandal hugely endorsed the nation's scepticism about their elected representatives. As well as being better served by the system, voters ought to have new ways of showing what they think. I find it rather odd in the twenty-first century that the stub of a pencil in a draughty village hall is still central to deciding the future of our nation. Forget BlackBerrys, iPads, and so on; even the simplest mobile phones are now centres of private communications. Let us put them to work to get better voting relevance. Of course there would be major obstacles of the risk of coercion and electoral fraud to overcome, but there has to be a better way than that illustrated by the appalling scenes in the 2010 elections, when people queued towards the closing time of a polling station – due to modern day busy lives – and were disenfranchised because there wasn't enough capacity for the last minute rush. Utter nonsense, and if a business behaved like that it would soon run out of customers.

***

A more fit-for-purpose electoral process doesn't, however, guarantee the quality of our elected representatives. Far too many MPs have done nothing with their adult lives outside the Westminster bubble – a frenzied, incestuous world where politicians, government and opposition, and the media cohabit. The whole circus forms a political class which is divorced from real life. Worse still, few MPs have any experience of the sectors of society which will be affected most by the laws they are making or repealing. Career MPs have neither served in the armed forces or police, run a business, commanded a classroom, nursed on a ward or worked at society's lower fringes, in our prisons. And yet these are the main constituencies which will be affected, for better or worse, by their day-to-day work in Westminster.

Some MPs provide good examples of the problem. These champions of the people come down from university, bypassing any real employment and slip straight into politics as a research assistant. They then become a Special Advisor to a Cabinet Minister. The 'SPADs', as they are known at Westminster, have a simple function – to inculcate party political ingredients into the attempts by elected and unelected servants to govern the country. The SPAD then resigns sometime before a general election and becomes the duly appointed prospective parliamentary candidate for a safe seat – and no surprise when they are returned on election night as the Member of Parliament for somewhere of which they know little.

That night they have achieved, under our current system, a job for life. The main job description is to obey orders, and not to make waves. The journey up the greasy pole of a political career begins, and in good time ministerial office beckons.

Whether Labour, Conservative or Liberal Democrat, these people come out of the education system, into the party machine, into a safe seat never having done anything else in their lives. Never worked in the real world. Never taken a risk; hired anyone; fired anyone; never been made redundant or gone on short-time; never worked in a school or a hospital or the Royal Navy or the probation service. And yet our so-called representative democracy sends these people to Westminster to make laws and govern us.

I am certain that when they arrive after their election they intend to change the world for the better as they see it. But they are quickly nobbled by the system. They are forced, on pain of being passed over for promotion or removed from the rungs of the ladder, through the formidable power of Prime Ministerial patronage, to vote on issues of which they or their constituents would not approve, and delivering opinions which are opposed to their personal beliefs. They have suborned the reason they went into politics in the first place because they have become professional politicians with a career to worry about; and they can afford to do nothing else. The party and its activists put them there (well actually, around twelve activists put them there), and the party comes first, second and third in everything they do.

Whether Labour, Conservative or Liberal Democrat, these people come out of the education system, into the party machine, into a safe seat never having done anything else in their lives.

That blind obedience is frightening to observe.

Come and stand with me in the central lobby of the Houses of Parliament as our elected politicians scurry to vote on an issue of national importance. The division bell is clanging, and the repeater screens in most corners of the beautifully fluted Gothic interiors announce a vote and the bill which is being voted on. Our elected representatives will of course be voting with their party, as the whips – the party enforcers – direct. They have rarely listened to the debate in its course through the House of Commons; they are probably not familiar with the arguments that the issue has encountered. The only reason they are there is because the voting process needs them to be there to cast their vote physically.

Indeed, they have often been hanging around Westminster for hours, always within eight minutes of the voting lobby (that's how long they are given to vote after the division bell starts ringing). This waiting time is often unproductive, an inefficient use of national resource. This is an antiquated system that denies MPs access to home life or greater connection with the real world outside the bubble, simply so they can stay within the eight-minute perimeter on pain of incurring the whips' displeasure and damaging a fledgling political career. Surely voting can be done in a more efficient way.

In democratic terms they are lobby fodder.

Here is the fifth largest economy on Earth, a nation which introduced democracy not just to countries, but to whole continents, passing laws through a system where someone with no experience of real life, elected by twenty or so activists, walks through our most venerated lobby as directed to vote on a subject of which they know little, or nothing.

Of course the major debates are well-attended, like the Budget, or the weekly Prime Minister's Questions, and of course a particular Member of Parliament will attend a debate concerning a constituent or an area of personal interest. Indeed, many an

MP has started, seen through and delivered legislation by assiduous, hugely time-consuming attention to detail. But most of the debating time in the House of Commons is attended by the relevant minister, the opposition's spokesman or woman and a smattering of MPs. And yet the sound and vision of this is transmitted into our homes at the press of a button. The armed forces can guide a missile onto its target remotely from a bunker thousands of miles away, and the City of London can move billions around the globe with similar technology in a nanosecond. Westminster voting should use something similar and similarly secure. If MPs could vote through that sort of a system, the need for them to be in London so often would diminish, they could do much more work in their larger constituencies and would, of course, need to claim fewer expenses.

Currently we have the worst of both worlds. The present system is unproductive, inefficient and misleading to the voters. We should either have voting in person and compulsory attendance to listen to the arguments in the debate or have party block voting by telephone. A refusal to change this vital part of our democratic process should have no place in twenty-first century Britain.

***

The career of a new entrant with aspirations to ministerial office also depends entirely on the patronage of one person: the Prime Minister.

Number 10 is omnipotent, even if it currently involves the Deputy Prime Minister in the Coalition, and our democratic system presides over the effective election of a ruler. The British people have a proper, working democracy for one day every five years and then they surrender all power to one person until the next general election. We have presidential politics whether we like it or not. The public think that Parliament is about Prime Minister's Questions, beamed right around the world as the height of intellectual parliamentary debate, a gladiatorial show piece between the leaders of the main parties.

Let's take it a stage further and have a direct election for the Prime Minister.

We moved electoral campaigning to the new heights of a personality contest with the televised debates of the 2010 campaign. But the electorate found out on election day that the 'Strictly Come Dancing' format was irrelevant to the voting process. You couldn't vote for Nick Clegg unless you lived in Sheffield or, more accurately, a small part of Sheffield. So the fact that a voter related to, or disapproved of, a prospective leader of our country, was irrelevant to the voting system. I propose a reformation of the system to ensure that it is in tune with what the public actually think they're getting.

The aspirant Prime Minister could be on a party ticket or not. There would be meaningful prime ministerial debates where the candidates would seek personal endorsement. The public think that way now. The media play it that way now. So it could work that way now.

We would elect a Prime Minister who would lead our country for a fixed term with no threat from a government falling and with none of the normal paralysis surrounding the leadership the year before a possible election. We would then elect a local Member of Parliament from candidates who, in the case of the main parties, have been chosen through primaries. The elected Prime Minister would have to govern with a democratically elected House of Commons whose majority may well be of a different hue to his own party. So the political issues and legislation would have to be won on argument and not rammed through over the bodies of the lobby fodder, by the strength of the whips. The country is aching for less confrontational politics. That is one reason why the present Coalition government is popular in the country at large. I also think that two terms of five years is enough for any leader. We have seen the damage that a Thatcher or a Blair can cause, not least to their own standing, by staying on too long.

Successful UK trade and investment promotion around the world is weakened by the small amount of time a British Prime Minister can give to the task compared with his French or American counterparts. I think that David Cameron understands this, but even he can't add that special ingredient – an official visit – because of our confrontational Westminster system that demands personal attendances. So often, UK junior ministers are meeting their opposite numbers to try and seal a job-creating, tax-generating deal for the UK in a country where last week our rival French bid was promoted by a visit to the country's leader by the French President. The latter didn't have to worry about PMQs and an opposition encouraging a press corps to denigrate 'overseas junkets'. This must change and a different type of Prime Ministerial office would help enormously in Britain winning more and more often in overseas markets.

The Prime Minister would form a Cabinet of some thirty people – not necessarily chosen for their political allegiance but for their intrinsic ability. To take an example from the United States again, Barack Obama adopted Robert Gates as his Secretary of Defense. Gates is a Republican. Obama is not. Gates had done the job for Bush but Obama chose him because he was the best man for the job. His political affiliation was considered to be of secondary importance to his skills. Both men clearly thought the country came first, not party loyalty.

The French President, Nicolas Sarkozy, appointed as his finance minister not an old political ally but a lawyer from a leading law firm, Christine Lagarde, who impressively knows what she's doing, an expert in the field. There is no reason why Britain shouldn't adopt the same ideal. Knowledge and expertise before politics, to make sure that the democratically elected administration is delivering policy through specialists who at least have experience of the subject in hand.

I applaud Gordon Brown for introducing the beginnings of such a system with the GOATS. Having been one myself I believe it was a forward thinking move. He took prominent people from different walks of life who had experience or expertise in a particular field and put them to work as junior ministers to add value to the delivery of policy set out by democratically elected Cabinet ministers. The Coalition government has continued the trend with the appointment of now Lord Stephen Green from the chairmanship of HSBC, to my old job at UKTI. The nation needs many more such people in areas of government delivery. Political careerists wouldn't like it, the believers in slavish party politics would hate it, many of the civil service would resist the change it would bring, and the media spotlight isn't for everybody, but Britain would benefit from a marked improvement in delivery. A prominent head teacher delivering education policy – now there's a novelty!

Of course all of this doesn't remove the power of Prime Ministerial patronage and the PM has choices over appointment or promotion, but at least the House of Commons would be more independently minded and, if some sort of qualification criteria applied to MPs, even after they were elected, to prove that they had experience of the real world of work (public or private sector), and were more in touch with those whose lives they affect by their actions, then real progress would have been achieved.

***

We must also start paying Members of Parliament a realistic wage. It has been unacceptable to successive Prime Ministers to pay them properly. So expenses became a carte-blanche method of topping up their income. They were told, of course, not to do anything illegal but they were shown the way the system worked when they first arrived and told to get on with it. It was a system which was wrong in concept, and foreign to any other field of employment anywhere in the land. The outrage of the British public was totally justified when they heard MPs of all parties wriggling on the hook of indefensible excuses.

The outrage of the British public [on the expenses scandal] was totally justified when they heard MPs of all parties wriggling on the hook of indefensible excuses.

But would many people have behaved differently at the time and in the same place and circumstances? Whatever people may say now, if you were to arrive in a new job, and briefed on the rules about claiming expenses, if you were told where the limits were and told it was all quite legal and proper, I doubt whether many people would have refused to claim. It was the system that was rotten to the core and out of touch, reflecting a deeper rooted malaise in our system of government.

THE BUSINESS OF POLITICS: FIXING THE SYSTEM

MPs' pay should be substantially increased and never again should they set the level of their own remuneration. Just as in any other job, properly receipted expenses reasonably incurred in the execution of their duties would be promptly reimbursed and nothing else. If they do need to come to London they should be accommodated in a decent not lavish hotel, bought by the taxpayer for exclusive use by MPs. They could either commute from home or stay in this specific hotel. If they were to choose somewhere else to stay in London then that would be up to them, but the British taxpayer would not bear the cost.

***

From reform of the elected, to reform of the massed ranks of the unelected who are nevertheless central and essential to the way the government operates: the civil service. We are lucky to have such a mixture of talent, hard work and integrity. From my experience, we have the most honest civil service in the world. They are very good at following the rules. But slavishness is not going to propel our country successfully into the competitive culture of the new global market place.

If we are to fix Britain, then we need to change aspects of civil service delivery. Let us consider three of them: government procurement, working with business and public accountability.

The public sector is a good customer for much of UK PLC. I am pleased to see that the work and recommendations of Sir Philip Green on centralisation of the procurement process and streamlining of supplier numbers seems to have struck a chord with this cash-strapped administration.

There is a European procurement rule which states that anything a government wants to buy, from a motor car to a knife and fork, has to go out to tender to member states of the European Union and what are described as 'relevant signatories of the World Trade Organisation's Government Procurement Agreement'. And yet, strangely, German ministers always get driven in cars made in Germany, French ministers are never seen in a car made anywhere but in France, British ministers get cars made in Japan.

We blindly follow rules that other countries blatantly disregard – and those rules hinder Britain, our jobs, our ability to attract investment and our tax revenues.

The Department of Business, Innovation and Skills has told me that 'it is not permissible to take account of wider benefits such as to the UK economy' when they are awarding contracts. It would be laughable if it wasn't so serious. Do we really believe that the French or the Germans or the Italians don't operate the system to their advantage?

When I questioned officialdom about our subservience I was told that if we continue to obey the rules then the others will eventually fall into line. I suspect that will only happen (if at all) when other countries have secured all the competitive advantage they could ever need. That will, of course, be never.

The power of procurement could be used to increase the level of skills of the employees in the supply chain. Why not bring pressure to bear especially on small businesses with 'I like your prices and I like your quality. Now, how do you train your people?'

We blindly follow rules that other countries blatantly disregard – and those rules hinder Britain, our jobs, our ability to attract investment and our tax revenues.

***

We need those serving our government at all levels – from central government to local authorities, from inspectorates to local planners – to work *with* the grain of business. The experience of British businesses which also have operations elsewhere in Europe confirms a very different approach there – look after your own.

Worse, in Britain the pervading unspoken attitude of the civil service towards business is that 'they're at it'! They will all say that they are not anti-business, but watch what they do and not what they say. Regulation is still seen as the first, not the last, resort. Many government departments and certainly vast numbers of politicians feel and behave as if business is for someone else, that making money just happens, and that exports happen 'over there'.

Every UK civil servant anywhere in the world should think of the ways which the private sector could benefit from what he or she is doing. This government is developing a programme of commercial diplomacy and that is to be welcomed. We have wasted a decade or two, and we have a huge amount of catching up to do.

Every decision which the civil service is asked to make must answer some important questions.

How will this help skills training? How does this help to create profitability of the companies concerned? How can regulation be reduced? How can its implementation be made less heavy-handed?

This approach needs to apply from a parish council level, through each planning authority and the Health and Safety Executive, up to Whitehall. It's a simple imperative – to ask how business can be made welcome and then encouraged to stay, prosper and create tax-paying profits and jobs, from any decision that any part of the public sector is involved in.

***

I'm not alone in saying that there are far too many civil servants. It's not their fault. The previous administration developed a system which bred them. The current shedding of back office jobs in the public sector, will see thousands of those who would have retired in any event not being replaced. The shift will not only help rebalance the country's books but enable the private sector to have access to labour previously denied. It has been crowded out by the enhanced pay and pensions on offer from the public sector, which it could not match. According to the Office of National Statistics, in September 2010, public sector workers were earning on average over 15% more than their opposite numbers in the private sector, with 90% of public sector employees having pension rights compared with under 50% in the private part of the economy.

My serious concern is that they are not accountable for their work in a way which would be familiar to the rest of the British workforce. A nurse is responsible for the patients, and a check-out person is responsible for the till. A train driver knows about red signals and an airline pilot has quite a number of responsibilities sitting behind her or him.

But not a departmental civil servant. If government policy goes wrong, it is the minister who is forced to resign, usually over matters of which he or she knows little, rather than the civil servant who is in full possession of the facts and knows precisely what is going on. I would have thought that our mature twenty-first century government has developed to the point where a civil servant who has done the work and dealt with the facts can be made personally and publicly accountable for it. If it's badly wrong, then the civil servant should go and not just to another department. If the public sector wants the pay of the private sector then it needs to accept the accountability and less job security that goes with it.

***

We are the United Kingdom, but we are also separate nations under the Union flag. Making the United Kingdom fit to compete effectively in Asia's century means we must consider some of the consequences of devolution. Powers were devolved to the Scottish Parliament at Holyrood but Scotland receives more from the UK tax take on a per capita basis than any part of England. It is a disproportionate and unfair deal.

The roots of the problem take us back to the late 1970s. It is called the Barnett Formula. Joel Barnett was Chief Secretary to the Treasury in the Jim Callaghan government in the late Seventies. That Labour government was hanging onto power by a thread and needed Scottish National Party votes. Barnett proposed, and it eventually became law, that Scotland would get 10% more grant than the maximum sum awarded to the English regions.

Scotland would get 10% more, simply for being Scotland! It was the price exacted from a minority government by just two Members of Parliament, and it has been on the statute book ever since. No party – not even Thatcher's Tories – has ever suggested changing it, such is the need for Scottish votes.

It is patently unfair on parts of England, especially in the north. The United Kingdom collectively raises the taxes from which regional grants come. But the wealth of our nation which can be divided up is neither earned nor distributed evenly, not even amongst areas with similar challenges but in different parts of the land.

So, at the very least margin of fairness, government grants should be distributed on an assessment of need every year. That may well mean that Scotland receives more than anywhere else sometimes, even often, but not automatically. A business in the North-East of England sees a rival just over the border in Scotland getting an advantage from the tax raised on the profits produced by the business located in England. That effectively quashes the incentive to invest and create jobs in the North East.

Another inherent unfairness in England's relationship with the Scots in a post-devolution United Kingdom has the potential to erode any notion that, in fixing our country, 'we are all in this together'. And that's the 'West Lothian Question'. It's a term coined by the veteran Labour MP for the Scottish constituency of West Lothian, Tam Dalyell.

A Scottish MP can vote on a subject which only applies to England. It's hard to believe that this is allowed in the Mother of Parliaments but it's true. But it doesn't work the other way round. An MP from an English constituency cannot vote on any matter devolved to the Scottish Parliament and beyond the reach of Westminster, for example education. But a Westminster MP from a Scottish constituency can vote on English education which is of no concern to his or her constituents but of crucial importance to England. It is unfair and undemocratic. The Scots wouldn't tolerate it at all if the roles were reversed, nor should they. Don't blame Scotland, blame the system that allows it.

We should immediately ensure that Scottish MPs of any party abstain in Westminster votes that relate to matters not applicable to Scotland, and the same would apply to Welsh and Northern Irish MPs. The United Kingdom is going to need cohesion to pull itself out of the mess we're in. This calls for courageous political leadership in every part of the House of Commons to restore a proper representative relationship between Scotland and England and indeed between Wales, England and Northern Ireland and the UK as well.

Scotland should be allowed to raise its own income and business taxes and spend what it raised on itself. The Scottish Nationalists would happily see the realisation of one of their ambitions but hopefully the penny would drop: that the country can only spend what it earns. Over time, the share of the public sector in the Scottish economy would decline and the private sector would thrive. Why? Because the devolved government would have to slash business taxes to compete and make it worthwhile for companies to settle, invest, generate wealth, create jobs and pay tax north of the border. Even the Scottish Nationalists must realise that they can't continue to be subsidised by a maxed-out English credit card forever.

As Trade Minister I flew to trade shows around the world, from textiles to food, from aircraft to mobile phone technology. I would often find that there was a stand paid for by the UK tax-payer for, say, the West Midlands promoting that region as a place in which to invest. Down the aisle at the show would be another from Yorkshire, then another from the East Midlands and so on. Not only did this multiply the cost but a potential customer could have struggled with the divided multiple messages and wondered where the UK actually was.

Eventually the English regions began to assume a more unified message. But not Scotland. Their stands didn't even fly the Union flag – merely the Scottish national flag, the Saltire. Once again, I wondered why domestic nationalism should be taken abroad, only serving to confuse potential overseas investors in the United, repeat United, Kingdom.

Economic regeneration in England is vital. The European money which has helped many of the poorer areas, like Cornwall, is running out.

The message to the potential overseas investor was diluted and confused and it still happens today. Now that we no longer have a Scottish Prime Minister and Chancellor I would hope that things will change. We need Scotland, with all her ingenuity, brilliant assets and fierce, justified pride to join the rest of the United Kingdom in marketing our country together. We are, after all, 'all in this together'.

Economic regeneration in England is vital. The European money which has helped many of the poorer areas, like Cornwall, is running out. The Coalition government has made a big mistake abolishing the Regional Development Agencies. They were overmanned and inefficient in many areas, and probably superfluous to some parts of the country. But making them more efficient and cutting their budgets was the way forward, not forcing their complete abolition.

Regional Development Agencies were independent of party politics. No dipping in the pork barrel of local preferment. A stability and consistency brought about by a business chairman or chairwoman and representation from all parts of the community in a region, with economic growth as the priority and not short-term political reward. I am all in favour of government cutting down on waste, but here it has reduced the drive for regional economic development at the precise time when it needs to be increased.

***

Fixing Britain constitutionally cannot be completed without changing the Second Chamber of Parliament, the House of Lords. It too needs to be made fit for purpose in the changed world of the twenty-first century. Again, unless it appears relevant, unless its workings and methods are understood by everyone, unless it has legitimacy, then democratic connection and the links between the governed and the governing that are essential to sorting out our country will not be achieved.

Very few people understand it. Not even Prime Ministers and MPs. It is a very British mixture of service, privilege, independence, stability and tradition. It should not be abolished. It has a very special function, which is very British, very subtle and, I believe, very necessary. What's more, it works.

And of course this subject is very close to home – I sit as a crossbench peer, not aligned to any political party and I am a regular attender.

Here's the first nuance. It has no democratic accountability, so the House of Lords does not overrule the House of Commons. But it can revise, amend, and delay. Which can often be quite a check on the House of Commons. But it does not overrule.

Of the 800 or so peers, 92 are there through family lineage. Until 1999 all hereditary peers sat in the House but, with the typical zeal of doing half a job and then moving on, Tony Blair abolished their right to sit, save for 92. This number does not diminish as each one dies (which would have been a way of removing hereditary peers from the House over a single generation) but by-elections taking place from within the hereditary peers themselves keep the number at 92.

Bishops take it in turns to be the living embodiment of the monarch as Head of the Church of England ruling the country through Parliament. They bring a huge amount of common sense and compassion to the debates. There are 26 of them. Then there are the party political peers – but they are much less slavish, and more independently minded, than their equivalents in the House of Commons. They number, and this changes regularly, about 188 Tories, 225 Labour, 75 Lib Dem and 26 others. That leaves about 180 crossbench, non-aligned peers voting as they see fit on each individual piece of legislation. These numbers show that the government of the day is never guaranteed a majority in the House of Lords, and so the government always has to win the argument in the Second Chamber rather than ram through a three-line whip, which is no bad thing for our country.

They all bring something very special to the party. I find my chance to listen and to participate in a debate in the Lords a treasured privilege. The Chamber is full of people who have done something with their lives. Bill Morris and John Monks from the Trades Unions, Andrew Lloyd Webber from the world of music, Barbara Young from the greener side of society, Patricia Hollis, with her expertise on pensions, Melvyn Bragg from the arts, Seb Coe from sport, Michael Bishop from the world of aviation, Robert Winston from medicine, My Lords Healey, Howe, Lawson and Lamont, all former Chancellors of the Exchequer, Colin Marshall and Iain Vallance from business and the CBI (two excellent Presidents in their time), John Browne who knows a bit about fossil fuels and funding universities and Eliza Manningham-Buller who used to run MI5. They (and hundreds more like them from former Chiefs of the Defence Staff to a children's TV presenter) provide their insights and experience for free. They inform debate and, unlike the bear garden and heckling nightmare of the House of Commons, they speak not only to polite listeners but they know what they're talking about.

But still it must change.

There is no room or justification for hereditary peers to sit in the House of Lords. The nation cannot be asked to accept great change and yet continue to have such an anachronism at the heart of law-making. The House of Lords should become a Senate, partly elected, with 100 elected out of a 500-strong house. They would be chosen along party lines and outside the general electoral cycle to avoid the same political sentiment colouring the make up of both chambers at the same time. But the other 400, which is an intentional 80/20 split, would be non-aligned appointees, adopted by an independent commission and not in any way under the patronage of any political party, nor the Prime Minister. They would be drawn from all parts of the public realm and would be non-aligned in political terms. They would have done something significant in their lives and they would be completely independent of political influence.

They could serve a maximum of three, five-year terms. A minimum age limit of 35 would apply with retirement enforced at 75. This is a wide enough age band to accommodate all the representatives required from society. This again would flavour the Senate differently to the Commons.

Members, except any forming part of the government of the day, would be unpaid except for valid, receipted expenses and would be expected to earn money elsewhere, always declaring all paid interests. Again this would constantly top up their experience reservoir.

The Commons would have nothing to fear about being overruled, the large majority of unelected members would guarantee commons supremacy. If the Senate were wholly elected then why couldn't they overrule? The Commons would not like that one bit. The Upper House would still have as its main weapons: revision, amendment and delay. The nation would keep hold of a pool of talented, mature, unpaid experience and the input of enlightened neutrality.

Existing members of the House of Lords could stay for one term in the Senate as of right and after that should, if they so wish, stand for election or seek appointment just like everyone else. Existing life peerages would remain for the holder's lifetime and future ones could be awarded as a huge honour for recognition of service to our country, but only elected or appointed senators would sit in the Upper Chamber.

***

Fixing Britain is not possible unless the machinery of law-making is modernised and made relevant to the societal behaviour of the British public. The nation votes for a leader in their hearts already. The public would be shocked if it fully appreciated just how its representatives are actually elected and then how they go about voting on their behalf. The House of Lords must also be relevant to a changed Britain.

It won't be easy. Vested interests and conservatism will fight for the status quo or look for a pork-barrel deal. We have a once-in-a-generation opportunity to change things forever and for the better. True leadership should grasp this opportunity with both hands, for the good of the country, the true democracy of future generations, and for the future prosperity of us all.

CHAPTER 7
TAXING BRITAIN OUT OF BUSINESS

As well as fundamental constitutional change, the government needs to transform some of its major policy areas so that Britain can build a prosperous and more competitive future.

We need to reform taxation, public sector spending, environmental legislation and planning policy. Research and development is vital for our future and we must also create at last a clear manufacturing strategy for our country. All these areas have a direct impact on the country's wealth and its productivity.

First we have to ensure that there is a wide enough gap between the money taken home by the lowest paid workers in Britain and the highest levels of unemployment benefit. We must make going to work worthwhile. How debilitating it must be for a young chap who has dragged himself out of bed on a dark winter's morning ready for another working day, to look across the street at the windows with the curtains still drawn. They don't have to get up because they're on benefits. It may be that they are getting more in benefit than our young friend is earning, but both sides of the street need an incentive to work. Iain Duncan Smith is right. It must pay to go to work. It must be seen to pay to go to work. Every part of government strategy in this field, from housing to training, must constantly have this as its theme.

We must make going to work worthwhile.

No one on the minimum wage should pay income tax. The first threshold for income tax should be £12,000 a year – costly in the short term, but so beneficial to the country as the next generation come into the world of work.

Child Benefit should not be universal – the parent's means should be taken into account. Why should a normally active, comfortably off 70-year old have a free bus pass? Or get a winter fuel allowance? The government spends £11.8 billion on Child Benefit, the cost of free travel for the over 65s is £1 billion and the Winter Fuel Allowance is £2.7 billion. Means testing could produce a decrease of 30% in the £15.5 billion total which would save the taxpayer £4.65 billion. If means testing is considered too demeaning then recovering it through the tax system could achieve the desired result.

When Alastair Darling raised higher rate taxation to 50p in the pound, his backbenchers let out hoots of short-sighted, anti-business revenge. In the total UK tax picture, the possible gain, assuming no lawful tax avoidance, of the new 50p top rate of tax would be a maximum of £2.4 billion.

Labour were delighted that finally the well off would have to 'pay much more tax', that the 'years of profiting' from a 40p top level of tax which was a Tory legacy from the 1980s were over and evidently the country as a whole would be richer. It was also good politics as poll after poll shows that the general public think it's a 'good thing'.

Well, the UK would not be much richer, as the figures show, and perhaps poorer in the long term. It was Professor Art Laffer – an advisor to President Reagan in the early 1980s – who suggested that as taxes increased from a fairly low level, then tax revenue would also increase, but as tax rates rose further, there would come a point where people would not regard it as worthwhile to work as hard or risk as much. If they didn't work as hard at creating wealth then tax revenues would fall. To illustrate the point, Laffer drew a curve which showed how tax revenues reduced with each tax increase. In simple terms, if take-home pay diminishes because of a bigger tax burden, production tends to fall, spending decreases and the black economy flourishes. The net effect of that is for the overall tax-take to fall, giving the lie to that fondly held and politically attractive assertion.

At some stage, wealth creators will pay clever advisers to avoid taxation – which is perfectly legal – or they will simply set up their businesses in another country. Either way, spiteful tax hikes increase Britain's loss. Only time will tell where the 50% mark is on the Laffer curve. Of course, it is really at least 60% for employed (as opposed to self-employed) people because of National Insurance contributions; an income tax by another name. So, currently, the higher-waged in Britain take home just two fifths of what they earn. Some incentive!

A flat tax, like Estonia's 21%, would almost immediately collect a lot more money, and fewer people would have the incentive to avoid it. Businesses would be told that there would be no fiscal reliefs or allowances, but in return their tax rate would be 15%. It might be, as in Estonia, that capital gains were added to the total taxable figure – but it would be a great shot in the arm for the nation's bottom line. But I can hear the howls of protest from the ill-informed opposition – at business apparently 'not paying their fair share'.

The government needs to be brave and increase the 'sin' taxes, on cigarettes and drink. Enormously. Tax on booze and cigarettes raises £17.8 billion – but the total cost of smoking and alcohol to both the NHS and wider society including crime and loss of production adds up to around £26.3 billion. In other words, the taxpayer is being asked to find, one way and another, £8.5 billion for smokers and alcohol abuse. In order to close the gap, the price of a packet of 20 cigarettes would need to rise to around £8.60. As a result we would have to do two other things. Costlier cigarettes will mean an increase in illegally imported cigarettes from the continent. We should make smuggling cheap cigarettes into the country seem the same as benefit fraud. The increase on liquor will enrage the Scottish whisky industry, but they will need to acknowledge that their real profits come from their exports rather than the whisky which is drunk in Britain.

The government needs to be brave and increase the 'sin' taxes, on cigarettes and drink. Enormously.

***

There is the smack of revenge on the taxes which have been heaped on our bankers, but it may be our loss in the end.

The banks must appreciate public desire for retribution. They must show they understand the world in which they operate when they continue to reward themselves very handsomely. They cannot expect politicians to look favourably on them when the people who elect those politicians feel that their money bailed out the banks, who then continue to pay themselves huge bonuses as if nothing had happened, when the nation is facing such hard times.

However, there are banks who didn't take a penny of government money, our money, and some of the leading investment banks in the City are not owned in this country and neither did they take British taxpayers' money. But here perception is reality. Each of the banking taxes have been brought in with glee by politicians and the public. If they continue to be treated like this then there is a very real risk they will base themselves, in four or five years' time in, say, Hong Kong or Qatar or Mumbai. They won't take all their operations with them, but a company is really centred where its head office is, and it won't be in Britain. Nor will their jobs, nor will the growth, nor will their taxes.

Leaving the UK is not something our major, successful banks want to do, but banking is the most international of business sectors. To remain globally competitive they will have no choice if UK domestic legislation prevents them from attracting the best people on a worldwide basis. The issue is one of maintaining a lead overseas and, if this lead disappears, then profits fall and, crucially for the UK public, so does the tax they pay to the UK Treasury. If people are happy to see these banks leave, then they must appreciate that income tax would probably have to rise to fill the gap.

Small businesses definitely need the banks to lend more on terms they can afford. But it is worth remembering that much of the finance for small business before the banking crisis was provided either by other, often overseas, banks or other credit suppliers who have pulled out of the market – or it was precisely the sort of risky lending that the banks should not have been doing in the first place.

**

If business is going to play its proper part in fixing Britain and also win through in its battle to recover lost respect (perceived or real) it must look at the level of pay increases at the very top of businesses in general. In 2009 the chief executives of the UK's hundred largest companies will, according to Income Data Services, have received 81 times the average pay of full-time employees. Up from 47 times in 2000. Performance and productivity has no doubt improved and we must attract the best in the global race for talent but bonus payments should relate to, and be paid over, the period the business enjoys the benefit of that talent and any advance remuneration should be subject to clawback provisions. Interestingly, no one complains in the same way about a footballer whose astronomical salary is paid week-in week-out regardless of performance. Business must come to the table of change with right on its side. It has nowhere to go if it doesn't.

Research and development is at the hub of a knowledge-based, value-added economy and UK-based R&D is vital if we are to win through in Asia's century. The UK spends 1.79% of GDP (£25.6 billion) on R&D. That is behind the OECD average – behind Belgium! The US has just announced an increase in its R&D spend of $100 billion ... yes, an *increase* of four times what we spend in total. The UK R&D tax-credit system works well (and hats off to some clever people at the CBI for putting that idea up to government) but much more must be done with universities and small, innovative businesses receiving special fiscal help. This is investment for our grandchildren's generation, not public spending with an horizon of next week.

At the heart of our business is transport, and our fuel is heavily taxed. We currently pay around 20p more per litre of diesel than they do in France. So our truckers face unfair competition from French lorry drivers who fill up with cheap fuel in Calais, work some loads in and around the South East and then when their tank is nearly empty, catch a ferry and fill up again in Calais.

In 2002 there was a proposal to institute a Lorry Road User Charge to ensure that foreign lorry operators paid their fair share towards the cost of using UK roads – with a charge set at 15p per kilometre if their fuel had been bought outside Britain. It was not adopted, but it could have been a considerable earner – the total distance travelled by foreign trucks in 2003 was 924 million miles, which under the User Charge would have raised £139 million and levelled the playing field.

Politicians will object by saying that the UK would be blocking the free passage of goods around the European Union. That doesn't seem to apply to French trawlermen and farmers blockading their Channel ports. The French have been fined twice for that, but it would be interesting to discover if the fines have ever been paid. We should insist on foreign drivers buying a carnet to allow them to ply their trade in the UK.

On the consumer side of transport, I applaud the idea of moving taxes on flying away from a passenger duty and into taxing the airline for flying the aircraft, because it incentivises the airline to fill the aircraft and to use the air routes in a way which maximises the use of the planes. But the government must also refuse to tax air freight. Global companies like UPS, TNT, DHL and Fedex have their European hubs at East Midlands airport, and have created thousands of jobs there with all the secondary revenue for an area that such activity and investment creates. If freight flights were to be taxed, then those businesses would simply take off, and base themselves elsewhere in Europe. Jobs would go, tax revenues would reduce but pollution in the form of emissions from trucking freight into Britain from the new hub in mainland Europe would not reduce. So it's a lose–lose; bad for UK revenue and bad for the planet.

***

The workings of our Export Credit Guarantee Department builds in commercial disadvantage. The UK cooperates with other EU countries to support overseas non-EU airlines when they buy an Airbus aircraft built in the UK, Germany, France and Spain. But UK airlines are not entitled to similar help when they buy the same aircraft. So we have the absurd situation of UK taxpayers subsidising overseas airlines (by way of loan guarantees which means airlines can borrow more cheaply), to buy and thus operate aircraft more cheaply than, and thus hindering, their own home airlines. Brussels says the provision of such help at home would be an illegal subsidy!

> **Britain prides itself in its openness to trade with other countries, but other countries often find a way, through taxation tactics, to make our overseas markets very difficult to penetrate.**

Britain prides itself in its openness to trade with other countries, but other countries often find a way, through taxation tactics, to make our overseas markets very difficult to penetrate. We need some fiscal imagination to give us an advantage.

It's time to fight fire with fire. I have often been told that any form of retaliation spirals into isolationism, sanction and reprisal – at the end of which everybody loses. Many countries continue to subsidise their exports and then, when they've made as much out of their subvention as they can, they repent. For example, let's take our old free market friends, the United

States. America's cotton farmers attract a subsidy of $230 for each acre of cotton farmland, five times the amount for a similar area of cereal growing. In 2001/2 that subsidy was worth some $3.9 billion. They will, rightly, point to subsidies that farmers from Japan to France and back again receive.

Meanwhile good old Britain pays a price for not bending the rules. It's so important for a small business to export either directly or by selling to an exporter. They need the help of a tax break – we only have a domestic market of 60 million people – we need these businesses to have equal access to the six and a half billion people in the world, with so many of them getting richer every day and able to buy our value-added goods and services, enabling us to trade our way out of our economic problems. We also have to make sure that the WTO rules help us export by facilitating imports from elsewhere as well. It would also help developing nations grow richer without aid; always the best way.

South Africa exports sugar to the EU who are proud to say that they are in effect allowing the import of South African sugar in the finest traditions of free trade. But the raw sugar actually goes into European sugar refineries, and the value is added to it in Europe, not in South Africa. If South Africa were to build its own refineries in Port Elizabeth or East London, and try to export its value-added product to the EU, the European Union would refuse its entry. Now in the roundabout way in which trade works, it means that South Africa is not as well disposed as it might be to tariff-free exports from the European Union, which of course includes Britain. So it's not just about fiscal stimulation in Britain, but also about making rules that allow value-added goods into the EU – so that the UK, which lives or dies by its exports, can in turn sell into more markets abroad. Not just because our trading partners would feel better towards us, but because such a policy would enable them to get richer and employ more people in a peaceful environment, which is of itself the great benefit of properly conducted international trade.

∗∗∗

Those value-added products can only be made by a skilled workforce, and a workforce becomes skilled through training. If we're going to ensure that people have sustainable employment through the twenty-first century they have to be properly skilled. Training is not cheap and one of the great ways of getting the private sector to do it would be to give them a fiscal incentive, especially small businesses who may not have a sufficiently large budget. We should make training compulsory, but small employers would get a tax break to do it. It would be a total tax loss to the Treasury of £4.86 billion, but it would become a huge long-term multiplier to the bottom line of the economy, because skilled and trained people generate so much more wealth for the nation and make our society a safer, healthier place in which to live. A 1% increase in the amount that a company invests in its human capital – its workforce – has been calculated to produce an increase in profit margin per employee of up to 3.66%.

***

The other side of what government can and can't do in helping to fix Britain is of course what it spends on our behalf. There are four areas where they have their priorities completely wrong.

The first is the cuts in education. No government can really afford to slice away at its teaching assets. In 2008 the OECD stated that the UK fell from 7th place in 2000 to 17th place in the world for literacy, and from 8th to 24th in maths over the same period. How did we allow such devaluation? Education is the ultimate investment that we can make in tomorrow, and we must change the way we do things in our schools and colleges, but cutting the budget is not the answer. The Schools Building Programme must be fully reinstated. Its abolition in the name of saving money was a grave error of the Coalition government. Give a truant-prone kid a new school to go to and feel proud of and you begin to change the way he thinks: you help teachers and parents win the argument.

Education is the ultimate investment that we can make in tomorrow.

Another major error by the Coalition is the abolition of the Education Maintenance Allowance. This enabled young people from very challenged backgrounds, who understood the need to get a ticket to get on, to go to a college of education, study on a vocational course and move on up. The abolition of the allowance may be a short-term saving but it is a long-term national loss.

The second is health. We all know why the NHS was ring-fenced from spending cuts by this government. They wanted to get elected, and the British people see it as 'our NHS'. It would be a very brave politician who was to suggest radical cost savings – but whilst everybody has an experience of how wonderful this NHS is, everyone also knows from first hand that the health service is wasteful and inefficient. According to the Office of National Statistics, productivity in the NHS between 1997 and 2004 dropped dramatically. It's fair to say that, unlike private healthcare and any other business, it has no control over demand or timing of delivery of its service. It can't turn people away at three in the morning, nor can it refuse a hip operation.

It is time that politicians were brave enough to say to the voters, let's see what we can do, let's see what can be saved. Saving money doesn't necessarily mean fewer doctors and nurses, it means doing things differently with fewer people who are not on the front line. And here's an unmentionable thought – should it be free at the point of delivery for the whole country? And why is that thought such a taboo subject? Everything the NHS uses, from its skilled staff to its sticking plasters costs money. The NHS is *not* free. There are patients who could afford to pay something towards their care – in return the NHS has to become more efficient and less wasteful. Patients would probably treat the whole organisation with a bit more respect and perhaps become a bit more careful about their health.

Thirdly, overseas aid totals £7.8 billion a year and has been another area of sacred ground. This government is, to its credit, looking at the money which is being spent for development work overseas, and already it has crossed some countries like China and Russia off the list, because someone, rather belatedly, has realised that they might not need the money but have been happy to take it. But what remains is the stipulation that British companies cannot have preferential treatment if there is business to be done with British taxpayers' aid, like building schools and power stations and other parts of a country's infrastructure. We cannot afford to carry on like this. Countries with similar aid programmes – Germany, France, the United States and Japan – all tie in their aid to contract awards in the recipient country. In such straightened times, why does the UK taxpayer's money – happily given to help the developing world – go to create jobs in Japan and Germany and not at home?

Lastly, even worse, is the threat to my old organisation UKTI, which is having some of its offices closed around the world. Every £1 spent by that trade organisation in promoting Britain around the world brings in £19 of business for Britain. There are few investments that give that sort of return, and it shows how valuable the rest of the world is to Britain's fortunes, if only we were allowed to maximise the opportunity.

***

We are happy to send aid abroad without strings attached, but we are in the unhappy position of having to cut our defence spending. We must make sure that defence manufacturing continues in Britain. We are world leaders in the sector, and hundreds of thousands of jobs depend on our international sales success in this vital area, let alone a contribution of some £6 billion to the UK economy every year. But you can't expect an overseas government to buy what our own government won't. It is important – and not solely for export success – that those who would have us give up making defence and security equipment do not get their way; our withdrawal from this international market would merely leave more space to be filled by the Americans or the French, the Chinese or the Russians. A well-policed, properly regulated UK sales regime is essential.

We must also make sure that we have the equipment needed to project our influence around the world. In the past, we've had politicians cutting defence budgets, but still wanting to behave as if we were the world power we once were. Sending our brave men and women into harm's way without the proper kit must never, ever, happen again.

Britain will need another Strategic Defence and Security Review for a post-Afghan-conflict UK. What will the Army need then? How should it be organised? Is the centuries-old brigade/battalion system fit for purpose in a future of asymmetrical warfare? Further restorative investment in the Royal Navy will be vital. So much of our trade depends on maritime security. So many different operations around the globe need a fully tooled-up navy. Politicians of all parties have come to believe that our capability at sea will always be there to be called on at a moment's notice. This is perilously close to no longer being the case. I don't think the public understand how scuppered the Royal Navy has become by a lack of investment. They are at the point of no return. There would be uproar in this island if the capability of our senior service was fully understood.

It's time to think the unthinkable and plan to absorb the RAF into the Army and the Navy. A future war is not going to be about dogfights in the sky, but someone in a bunker under the Nevada desert with his computer who will control his drone and attack the enemy by remote control. So aircraft are needed for very different functions today, and the Army Flying Corps and the Fleet Air Arm can do the job. The RAF budget in 2009/10 was £7.319 billion. If efficiency savings were achieved in splitting the RAF between other branches of the Armed Forces, we would save £1.46 billion a year.

***

We need incentives and encouragements for people to invest for their old age and their infirmity.

We must also look to the future. We need incentives and encouragements for people to invest for their old age and their infirmity. The country will not be able to afford to support its elderly as the baby boomers begin to retire. And even the prudent savers among them will have found that their sensible pension planning over their working lives has been debilitated by government.

When I was at the CBI, I witnessed such destruction of the private pension system. The assault on probably the most robust private sector pension environment in the world began in the early 1990s. But the Treasury saw private pensions as one of the biggest areas of tax 'leakage' in Britain. In 1997, Gordon Brown immediately abolished dividend relief on shares held by pension funds. Previously the pension funds, which held millions of shares as part of their investment portfolio, could reinvest the dividends from those shares into their investment funds, without paying tax. Brown reduced the value of those pension pots by £5.2 billion annually. An unnecessary swipe at an industry which is now struggling to meet all our requirements for old age – and as if that was not enough, he started to chip away at the tax relief on personal pension contributions.

The Coalition government has confirmed that it will simplify allowances and limits on pension contributions with an annual allowance of some £50,000. But, with an aging population, we need incentives to save.

Companies used to have final salary pension schemes, where the employer had an obligation to pay the retiree a proportion of his final salary through his retirement. It was almost an open cheque, with an open-ended financial obligation. Actuaries, whose job it is to calculate risk and life expectancy to set insurance premiums, could make some assumptions about how big the company's pension pot should be. But most of those assumptions were based on the life expectancy of retirees, who years ago retired at 65 and died at 67. That, of course, is thankfully no longer the case. There was never enough money to fund long retirements; it's just that no one ever lived long enough to find out!

But back in the eighties, the actuaries' calculations often meant that there was a surplus in the company pension scheme. The Conservative government of the day decreed that companies were not allowed to carry a surplus – some enhanced the benefits of scheme members, whilst many of them took what we used to call a pensions' holiday, paying nothing into their pension fund and also enhancing their profits. Either way, they were not allowed, by law, to put some money aside for a rainy day.

Which of course came. The slowdown at the beginning of this century and the fall in the stock market came at the same time as actuaries began to realise that the grey panthers were not dying at 67, but expecting to live a lot longer. So there was a perfect storm of more, older people enjoying a longer life, and pension fund managers lamenting their shrinking portfolios. There would not be enough money to go around.

Some pension funds went bust and the government decided to appoint a regulator. The regulator had omnipotence over how much money a company should set aside for its final salary pension scheme, how should it do it and when.

Introduced by the Pensions Act 2004, the statutory funding objective (SFO) requires that an occupational pension scheme that is a salary-related scheme must have sufficient assets to cover its technical provisions. It is deeply complicated territory, but this means the current discounted capital value of the future liabilities, expressed in actuarial terms. If a scheme does not meet the SFO, its trustees must agree a recovery plan with the scheme's principal employer.

When companies saw what the regulator proposed even more of them decided to scrap their final salary schemes – which had removed the state's responsibility for looking after so many people in their age and infirmity – for new entrants. The open cheque was being cancelled.

From 1999 to 2008 the amount of people in open schemes fell by 78% to 1.1 million. So over three quarters of the then pensionable community saw their pension expectations eroded. The law of unintended consequences struck again!

The regulator's funding requirements also started to stifle company's investment plans. Money earmarked for job-creating expansion had to go, on so many occasions, to fund a technical 'moment-in-time' issue. A fund would be calculated as not being large enough on one particular day and radical action demanded. But, a year later, rising stock markets or a change in interest rates could increase the fund's value substantially. Frequently, during my time at the CBI, I visited businesses caught in this bind. The pensions regulator was effectively running the business! Competitiveness was being eroded, jobs were lost. The essential basis for pension provision was a successful job-creating business. That constant law of unintended consequences threatened only decline.

Labour allowed huge financial responsibility for pension provision to fall on the private sector, but left the public sector alone. Alan Johnson, who was Secretary of State at the Department for Work and Pensions at the time, and Gordon Brown allowed people then working in the public services to retire on a state pension at 60 and only ruled that new entrants would retire at 65. Even the unions had been expecting some new phasing-in rules for existing workers which would have meant, for example, that 40-year-olds would retire at say, 63, and those in their 30s could expect to work until they were 64 or 65. As I said at a CBI event the day this was announced: 'What saddens me is that a government which has prided itself on delivering a stable economy has just mortgaged the country's future for £750 billion … 45 minutes of craven surrender have called into question the government's appetite for reform of the public sector.' Labour had thrown their paymaster public sector unions a huge gift, at an unsustainable cost to the rest of us. The nation can't afford it! Indeed, that same day, I was sharing the platform with a senior Labour minister who said (privately, in reply to my incandescence) that a future Chancellor would have to change the rules because they were unsustainable.

In one way or another 49.4% of pension provision for the over-65s in the UK comes from the state, from the taxpayer.

In one way or another 49.4% of pension provision for the over-65s in the UK comes from the state, from the taxpayer. This must be reduced. The state pension age will rise by one year in 2020. According to the government, £38 billion in today's purchasing power will be raised between 2016 and 2026 – £8 billion in tax from older people in work, and £30 billion less paid out in pensions and benefits. Imagine the saving if the state pension age were pushed up to 70. Obviously, there should be tapering provisions for people currently in their 50s and 60s, but people in their 20s now should be working until they are 70 at least. The age of 65 was set when the average length of pension payment before death was under five years. It's now over ten! Whilst the Coalition government has raised the state retirement age, it is not enough. Future taxpayers should not be providing a state pension to anyone aged 40 or below today until they reach 70.

The private sector needs a compulsory pension saving system rigorously enforced and a tax break which begins when a young person starts to earn money. Five or ten pounds a month saved at the age of 20 accumulates into a tidy sum 50 years later.

The public sector pension arrangements need some serious surgery. The official cost is £23 billion a year. I often wonder why a Chancellor who paid such attention – and damaging attention at that – to private sector pensions, left public sector ones alone when in the good times he could have changed so much with far less pain. The total liability is now somewhere between £770 billion and £1.2 trillion, which is the total annual output of a small country. A bit like ours, actually.

'Poor pay, but a great pension'. That was the justification for the public sector gold-plated pensions. Times have moved on. The average pay in the public sector is £700 a year more than the private sector. Pensions apartheid must stop. Public servants should have to do what the private sector does – subscribe to money-purchase schemes where both the employer and the employee contribute to each person's pension pot, which then buys a fund from which comes the pension. Public servants should be responsible for their retirement, just like those whom they serve.

***

Public or private sector, we have to tackle climate change and carbon-generated pollution. We can have a debate about the science behind it, the ambiguous status and expertise of the Intergovernmental Panel on Climate Change. We can have an argument about whether or not it's man-made or natural, or a bit of both. But one thing that is unarguable is our obligation to future generations. That we tried to clean up our act as effectively and quickly as possible.

We know that in using the finite source of fossil fuel, we must ensure that it will last as long as possible and pollute our environment as little as possible as we try to deliver a different technology to transport us, to keep us warm or cool, to generate wealth and to keep the lights on.

We have to develop more nuclear power, more quickly. Of course we also need a mix of wind, tidal and solar power, biomass, and carbon-free coal, oil and gas. But we could cover the country with windmills and at even greater expense put a solar panel on every roof and we still wouldn't have all the energy we need. Nuclear power has to be at the centre of our energy sources.

There will be no public money to build the reactors, so our survival is really down to the private sector. But whether those companies are British, or whether we have joint ventures with the world's leading reactor manufacturers, they will only begin to build if they are confident that government policy will be consistent over at least the next few decades.

The sums involved are huge. To supply 10 gigawatts of nuclear capacity would cost £15 billion. The first plant, with engineering, construction and waste storage, would cost £6.75 billion. The return on the investment for something like this has to measured in decades. So there will have to be some pretty firm policy guarantees in place if the private sector is to get involved. They must trust that successive governments will not move the goal posts. It is a vital issue for the country's survival as well. Security of supply is of paramount importance. I worry about our dependence on imported energy.

So the private energy sector has a principle role in our future. But the green agenda, which is ambiguous about nuclear power, is beginning to dominate business balance sheets with its enormous carbon emission targets. Britain's emissions are dwarfed by China and the United States – and India will step up amongst the pantheon of polluters when more of its one billion population come off the fields and into the cities as industrialisation of that country takes hold.

Brussels has been on a mission to make sure that European businesses should contribute to cleaner air and a decreasing use of fossil fuels. That is, of course, absolutely laudable, but prohibitively expensive and, in a globalised economy, uncompetitive. We should go there a little more slowly as we try to fight our way out of recession.

The estimated cost of reducing carbon emissions by 20% by 2020 is 48 billion Euros, which is 0.4% of the total Eurozone economic output. And the huge cost to each business of meeting those targets will make our companies less competitive. Whatever Europe does to try to maintain a cleaner planet will be of very small order, as Asia's huge economies continue to develop. EU governments should show they understand that the private sector is vital to our future, and needs to be given every chance to compete with the rest of the world, so it can help save the planet.

***

Planning is the fourth key area for very careful thought. We know that the planning process in this country can be painfully lengthy, but the major problem is uncertainty. We need long-term consistency. The private sector in particular has some very big expenditure choices to make over the next decade. It will be the leader in constructing and renewing our infrastructure, our roads and railways, but most importantly it will be called upon to invest £150 billion in low carbon projects.

As the CBI said in 2010: the government needs 'to deliver key energy and planning reforms' quickly, or it will 'risk undermining emissions targets and energy security'. Without clarity on government policy, £150 billion of private sector investment in low-carbon infrastructure would fail to materialise. This investment is essential for the UK to achieve a secure, sustainable and cost-effective energy mix that includes renewable sources, nuclear power and fossil fuels. The CBI said that 'uncertainty about the planning regime in particular is making investors wary of committing to new energy projects'.

We hear calls all the time for a greener, safer world, and yet we still truck far too much freight around the country.

We hear calls all the time for a greener, safer world, and yet we still truck far too much freight around the country. One of the busiest routes is the A34 up from Southampton docks to the Midlands – that itinerary cries out for a dedicated freight railway line. It would be safer, greener and, much more importantly, feed directly into the business lifeblood of the Midlands, the North and Scotland. But no company is going to commit without a clear guarantee that the whole project will go ahead. The timescales are immense – the Crossrail project in the South East which will speed east to west journeys across London was first mooted in detail in 1989. It may start running trains in 2017. And we want to compete with Germany do we? Let alone China!

The planning regime for business expansion needs some serious work. Imagine, at its most basic, a small business wants to build an extension. There will be the health and safety officer, the fire officer, the traffic department, the building regulation officer, the Environmental Agency and of course the planning people. My experience from talking with CBI members is that so often each of these (and many more) in isolation frequently lay down conflicting rules. Why is there not a one-stop shop? Planning for businesses should begin by asking how it can all be made to work, not to obstruct. Business can and will move on, and the local community loses employment and tax income.

Another aspect of planning which needs to change is the way in which indigenous business is treated in comparison with business migrating into the country. I'm very pleased that officials bend over backwards to help inward investment of course, but they need to use an even-handed approach regarding businesses already here.

When I was at the CBI, I visited the European headquarters of a large US multinational in Surrey. It is among the most profitable companies in the world and they have been a welcome addition to our economy for many years. There was something rather uncanny about their headquarters. The building looked busy inside, with a full car park outside. But next to it was another building with a full car park, but with no one in the offices. Strange! I had to ask what was going on, and back came the explanation that the original planning permission to build the headquarters had come with a specific number of allowable car park spaces. As the company grew in its building, more and more of the staff arrived, rather unsurprisingly, in their cars.

Public transport hadn't worked out a way of servicing this important local and national employer. This Fortune 500, US multinational, had to rent another office block next door, with its approved number of parking places, just to make sure its employees could come to work. Presumably some planning officer in Surrey is pleased with the outcome of that. If I were at the US global HQ, part of me would be wondering whether or not Britain was worth the trouble.

***

Finally, the UK must develop a manufacturing strategy for the nation. Fixing Britain will be impossible without it. We need to trade our way into economic success by making innovative, branded, quality, value-added goods and selling them around the world. In 2010 there was a marked improvement in our manufacturing performance. Increased employment and additional tax revenues are the result. We should build on this with clear, joined-up thinking and the settlement of an agreed strategy for all interested parties and vested interests to follow; it is that important. Manufacturing represents some 13% of GDP, far larger than financial services, and is more productive and delivers greater output than ever before in our history – something which is neither well-known nor fully appreciated.

So let us have coordinated fiscal policy to help training, investment and export, all geared to a template with definite, specific outputs. Let us incentivise universities, colleges and schools to produce more engineers, more technicians. Every planning authority, every government department must have policies which assist the growth of quality manufacturing. Let us produce more and better information that shows the way, with the media giving equal balance to good news stories as well as to the failures. None of this is difficult: it merely requires focus and drive ... and political will.

We need to trade our way into economic success by making innovative, branded, quality, value-added goods and selling them around the world.

When I was at the CBI, all the major pharmaceutical companies came to me, observing that unless the UK developed and promoted a clear strategy on their sector, then over time they would walk. They cited Germany as an example of a developed economy rich in business strategy yet, through neglect and years of poor government support and muddled thinking on approval regimes, had seen its pharmaceutical industry wither on the vine. There is never just one reason why a major overseas investor leaves (or, worse still, never comes – they're the ones you never hear about and thus cannot act on). The mood music created by our new non-dom policy cannot have helped. Increased taxation deters talent.

I thought of the non-dom row when I learned, early in 2011, that Pfizer, the world's largest pharmaceutical manufacturer, was closing its European headquarters in Kent, with 2400 skilled people made redundant, many of whom would have been non-dom.

There are two issues specific to Pfizer's sector: first the NHS purchasing regime and implementation of procurement and support policy is a real deterrent when it comes to deciding on investment locations. And, secondly, the costs of research and development are increasing with the risk/reward ratio moving in the wrong direction. Billions of dollars are needed to find a new drug. In 2010, global R&D spend by pharmaceutical companies fell for the first time in 20 years. So the pressure is on, as never before, for the UK to be attractive as an investment location for this, the most science-based and valued-added of twenty-first century sectors. The jobs it creates are precisely the ones we don't want, and cannot afford, to lose. But R&D tends eventually to follow the manufacturing. And both go where the market is and where the costs are lower, and where government policy and procurement support is clear and dependable. By 2020, China will be the world's second biggest drugs market after the US. As Matthew Goodman said in the *Sunday Times*: 'There are sound business reasons for carrying out more research work in Asia, where labour might be cheaper than in the West but the brains are as big.' The large pharmaceuticals are indeed investing in new research facilities around the world but the UK is not seeing them to any meaningful degree. 'This is merely a sign of things to come', says Goodman. Fixing Britain needs an emblematic, research-based pharmaceutical sector where public appreciation, government procurement policy, and a national strategy combine to ensure Pfizer's action will be a one-off wake-up call and not the beginning of the end.

***

So whether it's tax or planning, our defence sector, the environment, infrastructure or our manufacturing base, we need a regulatory system and a clear strategy which doesn't strangle opportunity, but rather nurtures our ability and our will to create prosperity. From that comes a tax base which helps fix our country – for the good of us all.

CHAPTER 8
THE GIMME SOCIETY

'Any fool can give the poor money. The question is whether money gives them freedom'.

William Ewart Gladstone, four times Liberal Prime Minister in the nineteenth century and one of my heroes, was right then and his words are still true today.

There are some shocking figures to show how millions in this country are trapped in a hopeless spiral of welfare dependency which fetters Britain's aspirations to be a prosperous world leader in the twenty-first century.

Half the households in the United kingdom receive some sort of welfare benefit. One third of them depend on the state for more than 50% of their income. When Tony Blair became Prime Minister the welfare budget was £90 billion. When Gordon Brown took over in 2007 it had risen to £160 billion, 25% of all government expenditure, and this was through ten of the most prosperous years the nation had ever known. Not years of recession when you could understand more people, sadly, having to be caught by a state safety net. The nation's welfare bill for 2010 was £192 billion! A quarter of all the money Britain spends goes on non-productive, negative expenditure. To put this into perspective, the Defence budget in 2010 was £37 billion. The money we taxpayers spend on investing in the next generation (the absolute opposite of unproductive expenditure), the education budget, is £85 billion.

There are 20.4 million households in Britain. The number of them with no one working has risen to 3.9 million. Of these, 841,000 are classified as workless because everyone – everyone – over 16 is described as sick, injured or disabled. What's more, 1.4 million people have been on an out-of-work benefit for nine of the past ten years. There are examples in our country where three generations of households have never worked in their lives – and that is during a time of plenty, over the boom years. There are actually two families who are known to have cost the taxpayer £37 million over those three generations. They can't be the only ones. Figures released by the UK government in 2010 show that nearly a third of households in Liverpool, Nottingham and Glasgow have no adults in them in work.

A quarter of all the money Britain spends goes on non-productive, negative expenditure.

A staggering 600,000 of 16- to 24-year-olds are not in education, employment or training. Youth crime costs the taxpayer £1 billion a year. Of course none of these figures truly reveals the additional cost to communities – the loss of self-respect, the loss of hope, the dull acceptance that a life on welfare and without work is the norm. And since no one seems to care, the motivation to do something about it weakens with each handout. Such is the birth and life of another welfare benefit statistic. The consequential crime, which always hurts the poor the most, has many add-on costs; and the resultant stress and poverty of health combine to add even more to the nation's tab through increased calls on the NHS and police.

By any calculation – financial or social – this is unacceptable in a developed economy that needs to compete in Asia's century. It simply must not continue. Moreover, we surely cannot afford it as a nation. Often I hear the cry that the banks – bonuses and all – caused the recession which has caused the need to 'cut welfare'. The banking crisis did indeed trigger the recession, and government borrowing has in part increased to bail out banks.

But the state or, more specifically, our shareholdings in them will be divested at a profit in time. The root cause of the need for cuts in our public spending is that we have been paying ourselves money we have never had and never earned for years. We borrow a pound for every four we spend – the sure-fire route to bankruptcy as every business knows.

Public sector debt in 2010 stood at £893.4 billion – that's 62% of GDP! Public sector debt in 2010 stood at £893.4 billion – that's 62% of GDP! So we are faced with paying people not to work – not to earn money for themselves and the country – with money we can't afford and which we borrow. The interest alone on that borrowed money dwarfs our education budget! With 670,000 households eligible for benefits and tax credits of more than £15,000 a year (so they would have to earn some £20,000 a year at work to be in the same position) it is not difficult to appreciate the size of the problem. Fixing Britain means fixing the basics and that means fixing what I call the 'Gimme Society'.

The concept of work is unknown to its constituents and its long established practice is to live on benefit. Over the past couple of decades government's attitude has been to say: 'there, there, we understand, have some money. And if you run out of money, here, have some more money.' We have ended up with a country where four million people of working age have never worked.

It is one of the mantras of politicians who boast about their wish to help the less fortunate, but the effect has been to imprison the recipients in their own, self-perpetuating poverty. Gladstone was indeed right.

When people are accustomed to receiving handouts as the norm they not only stop bothering about themselves, they of course assume that everyone else in their community is entitled to benefit as well so they stop caring for each other. Social cohesion is the major casualty. No one bothers about the old lady down the street, for example, because there's an assumption that 'they' will take care of her, and that 'they' are providing for her. It does nothing for community relations, and merely extends the perception of benefit dependency. That is not freedom.

The sad fact is that for years so many politicians have worked on the basis that giving these people money was the answer and changing that policy was a cardinal capitalist sin. It was of course, also, in the battle of perception a way of winning more votes.

We have ended up with a country where four million people of working age have never worked.

It is made worse by the depressing thread of the benefit culture running through the delivery mechanisms, from government departments to local authorities. 'How can I help you? How can I make sure you get what you're entitled to?', they ask. Not 'what you're getting is the last resort and only temporary. The benefit system is not a profession. Your right is to a

The present culture makes life very easy for the enormous unofficial but ingenious 'industry' which makes off with £5.2 billion a year of our money in fraudulent claims for tax credits and welfare payments.

safety net and you and I together will try everything so you can avoid needing this money.'

The present culture makes life very easy for the enormous unofficial but ingenious 'industry' which makes off with £5.2 billion a year of our money in fraudulent claims for tax credits and welfare payments. There is also the small (relatively) but important matter of £1.6 billion a year wasted by administrative error. With some 8,690 pages of rules for benefits paid out by the DWP it is hardly surprising.

A waste of money, a waste of resources, a waste of the latent talent of people locked in a system.

***

I interviewed a couple of intelligent but unemployed lads from good homes in Swindon, for the BBC's *Panorama* programme in 2010. Both had A levels but hadn't worked for some years. One wanted to go to college to train as an electrician but had been told that if he did, he would lose his jobseeker's allowance. The other was receiving £12,000 a year in benefit, which is the equivalent of being in a job paying about £16,000 a year. I asked him how he felt about doing voluntary work in the community in return for the money. He said he would, but no one made him. I asked how he felt about having his money stopped unless he took the next job that came along; he hesitatingly said he would but again, no one made him.

For me, this experience in Swindon encapsulates so much of the problem. These were not bad lads. They were bright, and not in trouble. They came from good homes, but their talent was not being maximised for the benefit of themselves and society. In the autumn of 2010 the Prime Minister laid out plans to change the situation. He said 'it simply has to pay to work ... If people are asked to do community work they'll be expected to turn up ... If people can work and they are offered work they'll be expected to take it.' Fine words and encouraging progress but, as always with politicians, watch what they do not what the say. There have been sanctions in place for some years allowing the state to cut Job Seeker's Allowance for 26 weeks if a claimant is failing to comply with requests. Even the government's own advisors admit it is rarely applied. So I am not brimming with confidence that things will change but change they must if Britain is to be fixed for the good of all of us.

It is ridiculous that the one cannot be trained for work because of a lack of funding during the training. Training is an investment in tomorrow for us all. Paying people to sit around doing nothing is dead money, unproductive spend. That must change, and quickly.

Paying people to sit around doing nothing is dead money, unproductive spend. That must change, and quickly.

Make no mistake, this will cost money in the short term, and at a time when the country can least afford it. But it will achieve huge savings in the long term, as is so often the nature of investment. And those who are getting no incentive to get back into a job should be coerced into putting something back into the community whilst they are receiving benefit. Clearly they would have time off to go for interviews for paid employment, but everyone would eventually benefit. They would be in the habit of getting up to go to work, they would begin to feel good about being part of – rather than on the edge of – society, which would begin to see something for its money.

We are in seriously difficult times which call for seriously stringent measures. Those who oppose a 'take the next job after three chances or your benefit stops' strategy say that it wouldn't work and the jobless would resort to crime.

I disagree. A few would (and the media would no doubt make the most of them), but provided it was worth their while I am convinced that the majority would begin their first jobs. There would need to be a reform of the tax system so that the gap between the take-home pay of the lowest paid and the highest amount received on benefit was significant enough for work to be financially and provably worthwhile, and recipients of the National Minimum Wage should pay no tax.

We would need a network of mentors and supervisors to support these new workers in what may be a very different culture for them and their neighbourhood.

Of course it would be expensive in the short term, but the long-term benefits would be enormous. Children would be brought up in homes where going to work was normal. People would enjoy earning money. Iain Duncan Smith is really onto something in using this once-in-a-generation opportunity to drive reform into our welfare benefit system. Her Majesty's Treasury will have to understand that universal cuts in the short term are not the answer when it comes to weaning Britain off its 'Gimme' drug. My concern is that today's politicians may not see the results in a time frame that suits their ambitions – but once the first results of this become visible, I think that many of them will be happy to say that they are planning for the long term.

The proposals to allow no household to receive more in benefit that the average earned wage is an excellent start and given that so much of the benefit cost relates to housing provision, society will have to get used to job and opportunity migration so that people become more mobile in their work search, so that housing benefit is seen as a temporary help, not a lifestyle choice.

***

The private sector has a vital role to play in all these changes.

Firstly, private agencies should be employed to sift fraud from genuine claims, with access to the government's databases of benefit claimants. Some of this work has already started. Many parts of the private sector do good work with 'customer facing' environments and many know how government works from years of experience working on hugely successful public/private partnerships. Their task would be a simple one – to give advice on stamping out fraud and error and they would take a percentage of the savings if they deliver. Checks, balances and controls would of course be in place to prevent overzealous enquiry or database abuse.

Claimants would be told of the conditions of their benefits before they apply. They would be monitored and investigated. There may well be some human rights protestations about this level of scrutiny, but the real argument needs to be stressed – that the sheer cost of the present system is something the nation can no longer afford. Hosing borrowed money at problems which hopefully will go away has been proved to fail. They merely increased, and we must now not only pick up the cost of change, but also price in the foundations of a better, more productive society.

It would also be helpful for local small businesses to get involved, perhaps with the incentive of a tax break, to work with some of these first time workers. Let's break the cycle of dependency. And the younger the better. Businesses will be presented with teenagers who can't read, who have never seen a live cow, who have never needed to tie a tie, who have no sense of right or wrong. They could be shown another aspect of the world of work and benefit from some of the experiences of people who have been in work for some time, and share some of the problems which they are finding on their journey into the real world. Don't give up! Work at it. Business, especially small businesses, must play their part.

Private investors should be encouraged to put money into schemes designed to help the country's poorest households. We *must* break the cycle of welfare dependency once and for all. Where criminality, welfare dependency and a lack of education is the norm, schemes incorporating early intervention can break the mould.

The whole field of welfare is not the prerogative of the public sector. There is nothing wrong with making money out of rectifying a situation that has blighted our society for years and which clearly is something where the public sector and politicians do not have all the answers. Those for whom the private sector's involvement in any of this is anathema, those who feel that political dogma should rule, should concentrate on what works, not on the tribal cant of yesterday.

***

In Wales I visited a school where a teacher told me that the girls were being encouraged by their mothers to get pregnant because that was the way to get a council flat! I have mentioned this on my visits to other parts of the UK and have been amazed at how many people are surprised that I was surprised.

The political dogma that implies that if money is handed out then change will follow is proven to be wrong; it has failed.

It is no surprise, however, that this is how people react to a system which allows them to do it, to get away with it. The political dogma that implies that if money is handed out then change will follow is proven to be wrong; it has failed.

Life is not like that.

In 1971, 7% of families were headed by a single mother. By 2007 that figure had risen to 20% – one in five. The UK has the highest rate of teenage pregnancy in Europe. If ever there were an issue for cross party consensus, then this is it. It's time to be honest and leave the political advantage of perpetuating the Gimme Society aside. It's time to build for the future.

Early intervention does work. Recently, the *Financial Times* highlighted a couple of examples: there are Family Nurse Partnerships in various parts of the country trying to help teenage mothers. Over the first three years of the child's life they try to wean the single family off dependency and into society. So far the lives of 4000 families have been helped by the scheme. It's been calculated that £6000 invested now saves £17,500 in reducing education failure and unemployment benefit later. It is expensive and time consuming but the benefits to us all are far wider than the money invested and the money saved. The scheme rescues the next generation from the no-hope trail.

My home town of Birmingham showed what can be done, investing £41 million helping families who were considered to be at risk from all the pressures of long-term unemployment, the drugs, the crime, the health problems. This was not a cheap solution but the scheme got in there early, kept on their shoulders, and put an arm round them in a tough but fair way. They were helped to skill up and be coached into a job, rather than drinking in the pub where everybody told them not to bother and that

In 1971, 7% of families were headed by a single mother. By 2007 that figure had risen to 20% – one in five. The UK has the highest rate of teenage pregnancy in Europe.

'the social' would provide. Basically, they stood a chance. It is estimated that the project saved the next generation of Birmingham taxpayers £100 million. Unfortunately for a politician with an eye on the next election or a Treasury wanting short-term gains, this is not a one year exercise. It's generational, expensive in the short term and cries out for statesmanship and long-term vision.

The sums do add up. The leading accountancy firm, KPMG, carried out some research for an intensive teaching programme for children with the lowest numeracy and literacy abilities. They found that if a pound was invested into working with a child who can't read, write or count, that pound eventually saves nineteen. The child becomes productive, works and doesn't do the drugs and the crime that so destroys the person, the system, the community and society as a whole. It turns out to be a twentyfold increase in the productivity of the young person – that's a mean statistic, but it's making a person into a valued member of society.

One of the neglected assets of the country in dealing with a fundamental shift from the Gimme Society is the so-called 'third sector': the charities and voluntary groups of Britain. They are skilled, experienced and well-connected in the communities where they're trusted more than government or the private sector. They should be used far more than they are, as valuable delivery agents in these challenging times. They know the problems intimately; because their resources are scarce they are neither profligate nor are they politically motivated. They are the best kept secret in the country in the field of welfare provision. Their money is one advantage, but their main asset is their people and their standing in the local community, their experience, their knowledge and their skills. Especially in getting their client base into work.

But of course there is a limit to what all these agencies, from the private, public and third sectors, can do. Parents need to shoulder the burden as well. There will be those who perhaps would care if they could, or knew how to, and there are those who simply won't. The latter are probably beyond help, but the former need some serious attention. Frank Field, who as a Labour minister was told by Tony Blair to think the unthinkable on pension reform, did so and was promptly sacked for his trouble. He has now been asked by David Cameron to look at these issues. He has proposed the idea of putting parenting on the National Curriculum, with appropriate examinations. This is not just about sensible sex education, preventing sexually transmitted diseases, unwanted pregnancies or about bringing up baby, but about the whole subject of parental responsibility on the journey through to adulthood. It will be aimed at boys as much as girls. Once the subject is on the curriculum then it should assume a proper importance.

One of the neglected assets of the country in dealing with a fundamental shift from the Gimme Society is the so-called 'third sector': the charities and voluntary groups of Britain.

These are not just issues for the challenged and poor areas, which most of the nation would rather forget. This is of vital concern for every region in the country, and included in the National Curriculum means just that ... nationally accepted as helping to deal with a national problem in an inclusive way; we are, after all, 'all in this together'.

***

I mentioned earlier the unfairness of income from take-home pay, not having a perceived or real advantage over benefit income. Gordon Brown's pride and joy was the tax credit system. The recipients had to be working to get it because unless they were in the tax system they wouldn't receive it.

There was some good in the tax credit system. It often helped those in low-paid jobs to be better off in work than out of it – without giving simultaneous tax breaks to the better-off. But it has caused large disincentives to people moving into higher earnings through promotion and has discouraged ambition for a better paid job. A company I know well in the West Midlands employed a woman in her late 20s who was doing really well and was set fair for deserved promotion. For the company she was a prospect for the next 20 years and she could look forward to years of progression, further training and decent pay rises. When the promotion came with more money she said that the extra would take her to a level where she would lose her tax credits, the amount of the rise wouldn't compensate for the loss of the credits and she would therefore end up poorer! She turned down the promotion, and ambition and ability went unrewarded, and it also harmed the business.

We can't fix Britain if people in work are being penalised by the tax system for working harder or achieving promotion. The first

£12,000 of waged income should be free of all tax. It should be available to those who are not recipients of higher incomes, with tapering relief available to ensure no one loses out as they rise through the earning bands of employment. But it would not be an allowance available to everyone's first earned £12,000; the Coalition government is wrong on that. Let's target it and its obvious costs to help those who are working but who wonder why, when the Gimme Society militates against them.

We can't fix Britain if people in work are being penalised by the tax system for working harder or achieving promotion.

If the Treasury says the country can't afford it, I say do the maths. Run the long term numbers. We can't afford not to.

We must create a meaningful gap between the highest benefit receiver and the lowest wage earner in take-home pay. That will cost more in the short term. But the alternative is frighteningly more expensive in the long term, in a way which has much more to do than with mere money.

***

We need to show, as a country, that we mean business when we talk of maximising the potential of the individual, rewarding people who turn away from the Gimme Society.

At the bottom end of society, locked away out of sight and out of mind, are some 88,000 prisoners. Some 60,000 cannot read or count to the standard expected of an 11-year-old and very few can operate a computer. In other words, they are totally ill-equipped to get a job in this globalised economy when they have served their time and come out, back into a competitive world of work. No wonder eight out of ten will reoffend within six months at a cost to you and me of a quarter of a million pounds a time. There has been some good work done by National Grid and their Head of the Programme, Dr Mary Harris. They started in Reading Young Offenders Institution and now many employers have spread the programme to over 20 prisons all over the country. It trains young men whilst in prison and then, in the last year before release, actually gets them working under supervision outside in the real world. These brave young people put up with all the teasing back in prison at night and are an example to the doom-mongers who tell them no ex-con gets work outside. And the success is proven by the fact that 85% of them do not reoffend and start making a meaningful contribution to society and to their own lives and the lives of others. Moreover, employers get access to a pool of enthusiastic, skilled people who are not going to let the employer or themselves down.

But of course before this visionary programme can start to make a difference, literacy, numeracy and basic computer skills are essential. Prisoners already lose their rights to freedom and privacy in prison and I suggest they lose another right as soon as possible: the right to refuse to be taught basic skills. Learning should be rewarded with extra pay and other privileges. Refusal, on any grounds, would be punished by no pay and loss of privileges. In twenty-first century Britain there will be no meaningful work for illiterate, innumerate people. To equip a young person coming out of prison to have a better chance of getting on than when he went in is an investment we should be making. Excuse the pun, but we are dealing with a captive audience! Let us use that to make it a win–win situation.

I have met some of these young men. They are not bad people. We should often look deep into our memories and ask ourselves whether at some time, if it hadn't been for a teacher here or a caring parent there, we might have been the one getting into trouble one night. Maybe we were just lucky. What strikes me about so many of them is that they are just ordinary people adrift of a chance. Many of them are very bright with untapped, unrealised talent which could be available to a business that bothers.

Business could have a role in giving the young person or the parent who wants to be free of the Gimme Society the leg up they need.

This might be for the young man who decided in prison to get skilled up, or it might be for the parent who wants to give her daughter a meaningful future. Small businesses in local communities could provide capacity and training – opportunity. The cost of this would, in the early days, be borne by you and me, the taxpayer. In the future we will all save on taxes not being given out as benefit or paying for the huge cost of imprisonment.

***

In the present dislocation of society's responsibilities, I can understand why young people join gangs. They feel, probably for the first time in their lives, that they belong. They can feel proud about something they feel they have a stake in. They give respect and receive it. They know what is expected of them and they have an order in their lives. I have discussed elsewhere how compulsory national community service can address some of these issues but a local business can also provide what a young man is looking for. Order, discipline: turn up to work on time – indeed, turn up to work at all, be part of something, identify with a wider cause. But for this to work, just putting the lad in the job will not do the trick. The public sector and the third sector must stay engaged, as should the parents. It needs all parts of the solution to succeed.

We are at five to midnight in this country and if we are to fix it we have no more time for focus groups, for listening to endless objections from the 'rights' industry. A truly cohesive and productive society awaits but political correctness and fear of offending have no place in banishing the Gimme Society. It will be expensive in the short term; it will require some difficult thinking and selfless behaviour from our politicians and many others. We must deliver work for those who genuinely will turn their back on a past full of rights with no responsibility. It calls for big investment of money, big investment of political capital, and leadership that we have rarely seen before in this country. Leadership is not just for politicians. We can all lead. Lead in a small community, lead in a school, lead in the world of work, lead in the public sector, lead in our sports clubs and lead in our society.

We are at five to midnight in this country and if we are to fix it we have no more time for focus groups, for listening to endless objections from the 'rights' industry.

This is not just an issue for the poor, the unemployed and the feckless. It's for all of us – the middle classes, the skilled, the private and the public sectors, the media, all sectors of our society. It's no use walking by on the other side of the road. The destruction of unskilled but meaningful jobs, and the 'there, there' cash handouts of unthinking socialism have created a frightening welfare dependency.

It needs a wealth, a prosperity of ideas to sort out the Gimme Society.

Business has a financial and resource advantage, and a golden opportunity to help in so many ways. Given the right sort of incentives, this is the time. The Good Samaritan could only do what he did because he had a few pounds and a willingness to make a difference after he'd made his money. Business needs to make the money, but its role in society goes beyond that.

After all, it is our generation who created this mess. We owe it to our children to put it right.

CHAPTER 9
OUR GREAT BRITAIN

In the summer of 2010, I flew down to Cape Town on business, and took in the England World Cup game against Algeria. That 90 minutes was so depressing and mind-numbingly disillusioning.

There were eleven of the wealthiest men in Britain. Eleven people who are heroes in their working environment. Eleven people who snap their fingers in their daily lives and legions of assistants and agents say 'yes'. Eleven people from modest backgrounds, now with riches beyond their wildest dreams.

But what I was really seeing that night were eleven of the poorest people in my country. Proudly displayed on their shirts were the three lions from England's coat of arms. The players in return showed only a poverty which disgraced it.

The England team displayed much of what I know is wrong with Britain today. Those eleven footballers, despite their incredible riches, could only muster poverty. Poverty of aspiration, poverty of inspiration, poverty of ability, poverty of teamwork, poverty of cohesion, poverty of commitment, poverty of understanding and poverty of will.

The England team displayed much of what I know is wrong with Britain today. Those eleven footballers, despite their incredible riches, could only muster poverty.

There was also a poverty of responsibility to the thousands of people who had saved, re-mortgaged, and given up their family holidays to come 6000 miles to see them achieve something. For themselves and for their country. At the end of the match, very few of the players went across to their supporters and thanked them for coming – they couldn't even muster up that small courtesy.

It was a dreadful sight – these players were well waged within themselves but showed they had little idea about their wider community, the people who pay their wages by faithfully turning up, week in, week out to watch them do their work, perform and win for their supporters' team.

They had failed to see how their sports community is not just about themselves, but about their followers, the nation as it happened, on that day.

Because we are all interdependent on the aspirations and the ambitions of the country, whether it's through sport or our general well-being and prosperity. Cohesion, through whomever or whatever represents our amazing country, is our key to the future, when many questions are going to be asked about our ability to compete as a twenty-first century player.

Cohesion and commitment, skills, investment, hard work and taking responsibility are the keys to fixing Britain.

Cohesion and commitment, skills, investment, hard work and taking responsibility are the keys to fixing Britain.

The footballers have wealth which very few ordinary people can aspire to, let alone achieve. But wealth is not just about the pounds and pence from a huge Wayne Rooney contract. It's much more than that; ordinary spectators of this game of huge rewards deserve to have their names on the team sheet as well, as we all play for Team GB and should all be pushing forward for our country's success.

I'm talking about creating wealth on a socially inclusive basis, which can be a game plan for everyone.

The Good Samaritan bent down, helped his enemy and looked after him. But he couldn't have done any of that if he hadn't got a few bob in his pocket.

My vision of socially inclusive wealth creation isn't simply about wealth as in notes in your wallet and change in your pocket. It's not just about the bottom line.

There's more to a wealthy nation than just money in the bank.

Without doubt, a nation has to be wealthy in the conventional sense. It must succeed in a fiercely competitive, globalised economy. And we can only reach out, down, round and under to those who are less fortunate than ourselves if we, as a nation, have sufficient material wealth. We need the money in order to deliver as a nation.

The Good Samaritan bent down, helped his enemy and looked after him. But he couldn't have done any of that if he hadn't got a few bob in his pocket.

So, we have to win in the competition that is globalisation and we have to earn our way in the world.

The only way to do that is to have a successful business environment in a democratic capitalist country. We need a competitive and simplified tax regime which works with the grain of business. We need civil servants and politicians who are onside for business, and don't act as if the commercial sector is 'at it' every day of the week. We also need to mould our role in a European Union to be outwardly focused to compete with the world, not looking inwards to take everything to the lowest common denominator, pandering to the forces of yesterday.

And above all we need an education system that pushes people much further, gets them into work, fit for purpose, able to add value to their country and themselves. As I said in my address to the National Association of Head Teachers' Annual Conference in 2005, 'Unless we educate children about risk, get them to understand it, to embrace it and exploit it, then we will fail as a nation.'

All of that goes towards all of us creating wealth. But there are other types of wealth too, which the combination of social inclusion and wealth creation can build on.

My worry is that, too often, political parties feel as though they are no longer elected to make public policy. Instead a few individuals around party leaders manufacture policies purely to get elected. Democracy is being replaced with focus groups and lobbyists, with no reference to the local voters' concerns. There's a powerful executive, and we can only observe its doings from the outside – MPs and civil servants alike are prisoners of a system that they either obey, or else cease to have a career.

One of the major problems that government is going to face is the tribalism which runs through our governing class. One of the major problems that government is going to face is the tribalism which runs through our governing class. I was very disappointed when, in response to the invitation David Cameron and Nick Clegg extended to the former Labour politicians Frank Field, Alan Milburn and John Hutton to bring their experience and their care for the country to help on social mobility, pension and welfare reform, the former Deputy Prime Minister, John Prescott, opined that they were letting down the Labour movement, accusing them of being class traitors. Prescott's tribal utterings are twentieth century speak. History. It's not the kind of talk that is consistent with what we have to do. We need to dip into the talent of the nation, and bring it in to help with these real, serious issues. Lumbering into the tribalism of yesterday will not help our children and their children. Surely country comes before party.

We need democratic legitimacy from those who govern us. It's not good enough in a high-tech, communications rich, media-savvy world, to have the old systems of placing an 'X' in a voting booth on a piece of paper every five years. People now need to feel they've participated in the laws being made for them, and that their vote has counted, not just been counted, and made a difference in the electoral process of the country and in the conduct and the voting behaviour of those they elect. Our education not only must deliver people fit for work, but it also must understand where our nation came from, and what it stands for. That must apply to everyone who lives on our islands, whatever their colour or religion. That calls for a wealth of confidence in our self-belief.

As a nation we have lost our bottle. We no longer feel that we do the business, and we need to have a generation brought up to believe that we can deliver. Not in the projection of military or economic power alone, but in the promotion of our essential tenets of freedom – of assembly, of speech, of worship. We are an open society, and we should say to the rest of the world: if you speak English and you have a skill, and you're prepared to work hard and integrate, regardless of the god you worship or the colour of your skin, then you are welcome. And if you liked our way of life enough to up sticks and come here, then help us maintain what you found attractive.

Our education not only must deliver people fit for work, but it also must understand where our nation came from, and what it stands for.

But if you are not prepared to learn or speak English and you are not prepared to integrate, then this country isn't for you.

I remember back in Birmingham in the nineties, the council decided it was not going to mark the usual Christmas, but instead it 'celebrated' what it described as 'Winterval', because it didn't want to offend non-believers in the Christmas story.

Such action is so destructive of the very cohesion we must develop. It turns people against immigrant communities needlessly and often such decisions emanate from ideas promulgated by non-immigrants rather than ethnic communities who frankly couldn't be bothered as they just get on with their everyday new lives. If we are going to have self-belief and understanding in our country then the authorities must not pander to a multiculturalism which has plainly become divisive, militating against us being able to pull together as one nation.

In all this, business has a role in giving a leg up to those who can't, who aren't able. People like working for companies which wear the corporate social responsibility badge on their sleeves. People like buying products and services from them. What's more, it is simply the right thing to do. If business is going to be allowed to prosper, if it's going to be cut some slack in taxation and regulation, then business in return has to be better at regulating itself, has to step up to the plate on training and at the same time practice good corporate governance.

At the CBI, in the early years of this century I fought hard and successfully against making corporate social responsibility (CSR) a legal obligation for businesses, because the moment you make something law, it moves out of the human resource, externally focused offices and into the finance director's office, with the words 'make this cost us as little as possible'.

I don't want CSR to have the same status as the upgrade of the firm's toilets or a new bit of machinery. I want it to be in the DNA of a business. I want people to understand that these are the values of a business, and if you join this business, deal with this business, this is what you buy into.

In the course of an apprenticeship or the beginning of a career, you would be asked to do your bit in the hospital wards or the hospice kitchens, or with an environmental project or with wounded soldiers. It's not about giving money, it's about giving your enthusiasm, your leadership, your inspiration and your time.

If it's not mandatory, but comes out of a wish of the company, the younger employees will quite enjoy it, they will feel that they are in a business which cares.

They will feel they are making a difference because they want to.

We have to make sure that the smallest business does it as well as the largest one.

If we take just a minute and look around us, we all have someone whose life we can improve, whose talent we can maximise, whose self-belief we can increase by what we do, not by what we say alone. Now that is leadership.

Fixing Britain calls for leadership. Leading isn't something which is left to the boss, be it the Prime Minister or head teacher. Each one of us has a responsibility to lead, to set an example, to encourage and inspire, to be there for other people.

If we take just a minute and look around us, we all have someone whose life we can improve, whose talent we can maximise, whose self-belief we can increase by what we do, not by what we say alone. Now that is leadership.

On 22 November, 2003 in the Telstra Stadium in Sydney, England went head to head with the host nation in the Rugby World Cup Final. Martin Johnson was the captain. He told me later that as he marched his players out from the dressing room, they were standing waiting to be cheered onto the pitch at the start of the game, and he looked back down the line of the other fourteen, minded to say some last few words of encouragement.

He looked them in the eye, and realised that he had no need to say anything. They knew exactly what they had to do. In amongst the team were seven or eight club captains, men who led their teams out every Saturday back in England, having regularly inspired their teams to go beyond what they thought they could do.

These captains, just like Nelson's, were masters of their own ships, but their joint Trafalgar had been drawn up on a different canvas. Each of them knew where their responsibility lay. Sir Clive Woodward, the coach, had prepared them superbly. Martin Johnson's task was to take them a stage further.

Anybody who takes responsibility for their own actions is a leader.

This is a very good example of the essence of leadership: that you take people to places that they didn't feel they could go and you enable them to achieve things they didn't feel able to achieve. Everyone can get there. It takes a leader who understands motivation. And that sort of leadership builds self-belief and can make everyone a leader.

There are those leaders who reach the top of the pile and who, in the rawest sense, get 20 men to follow them up a hill into fatal gunfire or, in Nelson's day, into the huge French and Spanish fleet at Trafalgar. That may be for the very few, but those who do anything whose actions affect somebody else, lead.

Anybody who takes responsibility for his or her own actions is a leader.

Indeed, I've wondered so many times over the recent years what it actually takes to resign. What it takes in the public sector to accept accountability and responsibility and in the private sector what it takes for someone not to be rewarded for failure.

But leadership is also built on the feeling that what you do matters. The example you set and the responsibility you take. These are big places to go for many people. But if you have those abilities, it is incumbent upon you to pass them on. Imbue self-belief and inspiration in others. Do as you would be done by. If you decide to take the role, then encourage people to ask why, and don't shout at them when they do. Explain why and you help them understand. Then they will buy into what you're trying to achieve. But in the end, the most important thing is to give people self-belief.

Martin Johnson managed that task with his team of captains and players. Business should learn from it and take it as their responsibility to make it work.

In a much more important and vital way, Churchill gave Britain self-belief in those darkest days of 1940. Britain was completely alone, with few aircraft, a fleet somewhere at sea and with hundreds of thousands of our army retreating from France. Retreat, for whatever reason, was not something our nation was used to.

I imagine him sitting in 10 Downing Street, and thinking that, in a couple of months' time, the Nazis were going to be over the Channel. His words, broadcast to the nation are familiar and are wonderful:

> *We shall go on to the end, we shall fight in France,*
> *we shall fight on the seas and oceans,*
> *we shall fight with growing confidence and growing strength in*
> *the air, we shall defend our Island, whatever the cost may be,*
> *we shall fight on the beaches,*
> *we shall fight on the landing grounds,*
> *we shall fight in the fields and in the streets,*
> *we shall fight in the hills;*
> *we shall never surrender*

Churchill was trying to encourage a country that hadn't been ready for this, didn't feel it could do it, with its armed forces fresh in retreat off the beaches of Dunkirk, tail between its legs – and he had to persuade Britain that they had it in them to fight. And we were alone. No Americans, no Russians. We were utterly and completely alone.

He pulled it off. He got them to believe.

As did a famous England football manager, long before the multimillion pound contracts of today's players. 'You've won it once, now go out and win it again', said Alf Ramsey to eleven tired, drained and acutely disappointed England footballers after ninety minutes of the 1966 World Cup Final. Victory had been taken from them in the last minute of normal time. Extra time beckoned. Exhausted, disappointed, but the players, inspired and full of renewed hope, delivered.

He pulled it off. He got them to believe.

Martin Johnson in that last minute of extra time in the 2003 Rugby World Cup Final, pulled it off. He got them to believe.

It is important in a Britain fit for purpose that we develop as a nation with self-confidence. A self-confidence not born of the arrogance of which we've always been accused. Because we were a colonial power, we were the old empire, we will always be accused of being arrogant even if we aren't.

I think it's more about self-confidence. How is it that Manchester United and Chelsea often win their matches in the last minutes of the game? It's because they have this amazing ability to believe in themselves.

I am one of the directors and shareholders in Leicester Tigers. The team also wins many games in those final seconds because they believe that they can and, most importantly, they've done it before. They are confident in their ability. They are confident about handling the pressure. They look out for each other. The members of the team help one another. They lead each other on the field. They keep playing down to the final whistle. So many teams give up before the end, subconsciously but fatally believing that they can coast down to the final whistle. But the best teams know how to win in the last minute. They play past it.

Knowing how to win is part of this, having the confidence that it will come good in the end.

It is important in a Britain fit for purpose that we develop as a nation with self-confidence. A self-confidence not born of the arrogance of which we've always been accused.

And that's what we have to do as the United Kingdom. We have to ensure that this great nation, that's equipped in so many ways to make the next two decades our own, delivers on its ability, maximising its talent. We can leave the race to be the biggest economy in the world to the Chinese and the Americans. We can leave the race to be the biggest in military terms to others, but as a nation we are eminently equipped to maximise the talent of our people, use the globalised economy as our home market … and win

***

And our people will be living for a very long time.

If you're 20, you're looking at a possible lifespan of another 70 years. Your children are going to find nothing remarkable about living beyond 100. There will no longer be telegrams from the King when you've done the ton, there might not even be telegrams at 110. People will want to work in their 70s and their 80s. They won't do the same job, and may work part time, or they might want to do voluntary work instead, but they will want to be active and participative members of our communities.

This world today of the twenty-year old, and his or her child, is completely different from the world when I was serving behind the counter in Alvechurch, when I was fighting for business at the CBI, and even when I was going round the world banging the drum for UK trade and investment.

There are some things that this generation must do now if we are going to give the next one a chance. For the good of our country, this nation which saw off the Spanish Armada, Napoleon and Hitler; this nation which gave the world a common language; this nation which has a reputation around the world for being a bit slow, a bit patronising – but actually good to deal with, open and with a tremendous sense of fairness; we must give our children a future they can afford and, above all else, an education and the skills that equip them to deal with this very uncertain world.

We must ensure that our openness and our natural sense of tolerance is not abused, and not taken for granted. We must leave our children with a sustainable environment that can withstand the pressures of commercial energy and transport development which, in time, leaves us in a competitive state so that there will actually be an economy which we can be green about.

We must ensure that the nation's faith in an elected parliament is bolstered by public acknowledgement of its supremacy and sovereignty over the unelected, unaccountable officials, commissioners and judges of the European Commission and Court of Human Rights. The pendulum must swing back to the centre and balance be restored, if a place where common sense and the wish of the people is to prevail. Let's renew our confidence in ourselves.

We also need to make these future generations aware of where they came from, imbue in them an assumption of responsibility not just for their own actions, but also as part of this great nation. Great nations self-improve. We mustn't be satisfied with where we've reached. We need to reach on and reach further – never settling for the now, but being restless for more success tomorrow.

Let's release the talent of the nation.

We are not owed anything. Not respect. Not a living. Not a future. It all has to be earned. No escape, no blaming others.

This is just too important.

Remember, it wasn't the Hun coming through the Ardennes Forest or the Scot coming over Hadrian's Wall that did for Rome.

Rome did for Rome.

I don't want that to happen to my country, our country.

ACKNOWLEDGEMENTS

Thanks to KPMG in the UK for providing some statistics.

Thanks to Michael Wilson, without whose advice and patience this whole project just would not have flown.

INDEX